Editor: Ben Jones
Production editor: Ian Barnsley
Designer: Lucy Carnell, atg-media.com
Cover design: Kelvin Clements
Advertising manager: Sue Keily
Publisher: Steve O'Hara
Publishing director: Dan Savage
Commercial director: Nigel Hole
Marketing manager: Charlotte Park
cpark@mortons.co.uk

Printed by: William Gibbons & Sons,
Wolverhampton
ISBN: 978-1-911276-72-2

Published by:
Mortons Media Group Ltd, Media Centre,
Morton Way, Horncastle, Lincolnshire LN9 6JR
Tel: 01507 529529

Copyright
Mortons Media Group Ltd, 2018
All rights reserved.

MORTONS
MEDIA GROUP LTD

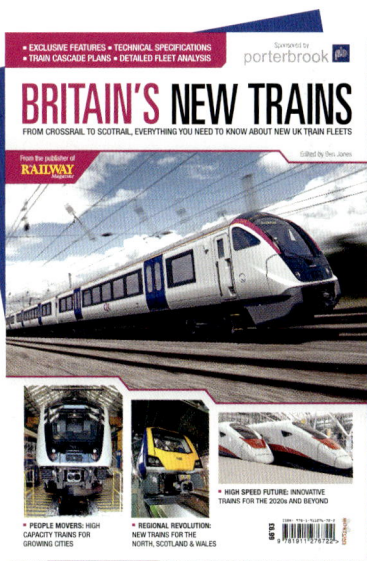

● EXCLUSIVE FEATURES ● TECHNICAL SPECIFICATIONS
● TRAIN CASCADE PLANS ● DETAILED FLEET ANALYSIS

Sponsored by
porterbrook

BRITAIN'S NEW TRAINS
FROM CROSSRAIL TO SCOTRAIL, EVERYTHING YOU NEED TO KNOW ABOUT NEW UK TRAIN FLEETS

From the publisher of
RAILWAY

Edited by Ben Jones

● PEOPLE MOVERS: HIGH
CAPACITY TRAINS FOR
GROWING CITIES
● REGIONAL REVOLUTION:
NEW TRAINS FOR THE
NORTH, SCOTLAND & WALES
● HIGH SPEED FUTURE: INNOVATIVE
TRAINS FOR THE 2020s AND BEYOND

CW01391548

WELCOME...

" I am delighted that Porterbrook is able
to work with Ben and the Mortons team
to bring you this excellent reference volume
on the new trains soon to serve Britain's railway.

Our industry is growing and the railways are carrying more
passengers than ever before. I am proud to say that Porterbrook
has played a critical role in engineering this success. Over the
last 24 years we have invested more than £3 billion in new
rolling stock and introduced more than 4500 new locomotives,
passenger and freight vehicles into service.

Today, Porterbrook accounts for 32% of the overall leased
passenger fleet on the UK network, which means our trains
safely carry more than 1.5 million passengers a day.

That said, there are challenges ahead. Passengers, freight
users and stakeholders rightly demand that we focus on
performance and delivery. This is a challenge to which both the
infrastructure and rolling stock supply chain must step up.

For its part, Porterbrook is committed to working
collaboratively and in partnership with our supply chain –
whether that be for new-build or refurbished fleets. By keeping
an absolute focus on day-to-day delivery, as well as on the
future needs of passengers, we can help the railway to succeed
and grow.

I am confident that by working together we can do this and,
as a sign of that confidence, Porterbrook is looking to invest
£1bn in UK rail over the next five years.

**Mary Grant, chief executive officer,
Porterbrook Leasing**

porterbrook

CONTENTS

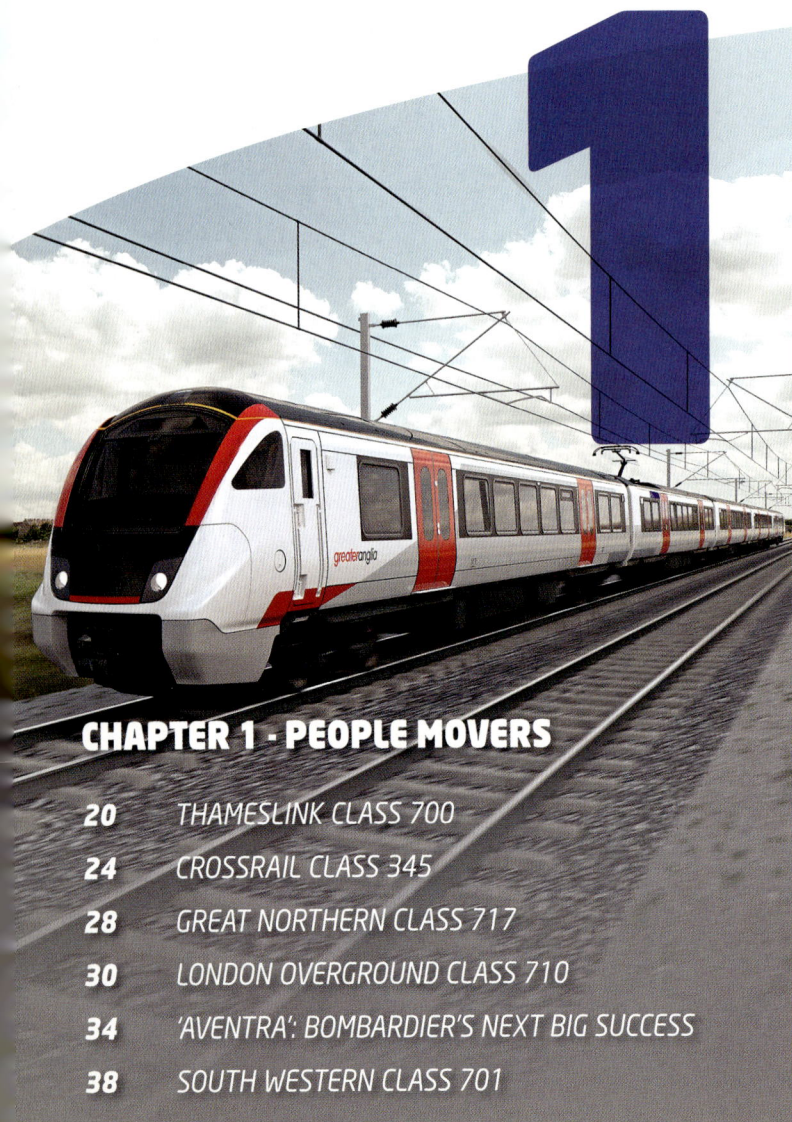

1

CHAPTER 1 - PEOPLE MOVERS

CHAPTER 2
NEW GENERATION INTER-CITY

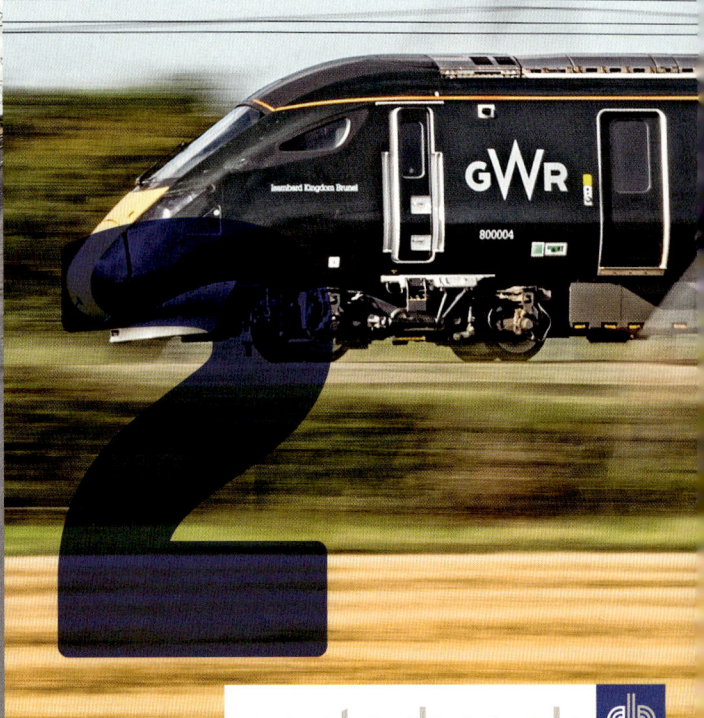

2

porterbrook

CHAPTER 3 REGIONAL REVOLUTION

CHAPTER 4 EXTENDING ASSET LIFE

porterbrook

BRIDGE TO THE FUTURE

After many years of arguments, negotiations, design and testing, passengers are now starting to see new Intercity Express Programme (IEP) trains entering service on major routes. Great Western Railway's Class 800s started work in October 2017 and East Coast Main Line passengers will get their first taste of the new generation in December this year. During testing to clear the type for use over more than 1700 miles of regular and diversionary routes, a Virgin-liveried nine-car Class 800 crosses the Royal Border Bridge at Berwick-upon-Tweed.
GEOFF GRIFFITHS

porterbrook

LONDON'S NEW EAST-WEST ARTERY

When it opens to passengers in December, Crossrail will revolutionise travel across London, providing fast links from Shenfield, Abbey Wood and Canary Wharf in the east via the City of London and the West End to Heathrow and the Thames Valley by December 2019. Bombardier is building 70 new nine-car 'Aventra' EMUs to work the services, branded 'Elizabeth Line' by Transport for London. CROSSRAIL

porterbrook

331 101

CAF

n north

porterbrook

NEW LOOK FOR NORTHERN

CAF of Spain is building 43 electric trains and 55 diesel units (281 vehicles) for Arriva Northern, which will allow the withdrawal of many older trains, such as the unpopular Class 142/144 'Pacer' railbuses dating from the mid-1980s and an increase in capacity on many routes. However, before they start working in northern England, the trains are to undergo an extensive test programme across Europe. Four-car EMU No. 331101 was undergoing dynamic testing at the Velim test centre in the Czech Republic on May 3. QUINTUS VOSMAN

porterbrook

GREATER ANGLIA FLIRTS WITH BI-MODES

For its regional routes across East Anglia, Abellio Greater Anglia is taking delivery of 38 bi-mode (diesel/25kv AC electric) FLIRT trains from Stadler of Switzerland. Built using components manufactured in Hungary, Poland and Switzerland, the innovative trains will start to arrive in the UK later this year and will replace Class 153, 156 and 170 DMUs from 2019. GREATER ANGLIA

porterbrook

greateranglia

STADLER

porterbrook

Left: A member of Britain's most reliable passenger train fleet, Porterbrook-owned 'Desiro' No. 350252, races through a deserted Tile Hill station near Coventry with a London Northwestern Railway service from Euston to Birmingham New Street on December 10, 2017. This was the new operator's first day in charge of West Coast Main Line and West Midlands regional services, and the day it announced that the '350/2s' would be replaced by new EMUs from 2021/22. FRASER PITHIE

A gaggle of South Western Railway Class 455 and 456 EMUs await their next sortie into the suburbs of south-west London at Waterloo on June 20, 2017. All these Porterbrook-owned trains will be replaced in 2019/20, and the company is currently looking at various options for cascading them to other operators on the third-rail network or modifying them for use elsewhere. EIKI SEKINE

porterbrook

ENGINEERING SOLUTIONS
FOR A CHANGING
RAIL INDUSTRY

Ben Jones talks to Stephen McGurk, chief commercial officer of rolling stock company Porterbrook to find out more about how the company plans to invest £1 billion in the UK rail industry over the next five years.

O ver the last decade more and more passengers have been using Britain's railways to commute into our big cities or for leisure travel. The extra pressure this has placed on a network with Victorian origins has created a huge challenge for Network Rail and train operators alike.

Complaints about overcrowding, delays and unreliable services have been on the rise for several years. Couple that with a generation of ex-British Rail trains coming to the end of their working lives and the need for new trains becomes very clear.

By 2021, more than 7000 new vehicles will have been introduced by train operators across the country – as many as in the previous 20 years combined. While many will replace older trains such as the Class 142-144 'Pacers' and iconic InterCity 125s, others will add much-needed extra capacity on routes such as Thameslink and Crossrail, but many thousands of good quality vehicles will also be looking for new homes. The latest estimates suggest that more than 5000 existing passenger vehicles will be displaced by 2022. Some have

been snapped up by eager operators, but at least 50 miles of secure storage sidings will be required to stable the rest, should they all go off-lease.

According to the Rail Delivery Group (RDG), the new vehicles "represent an investment of at least £13.8bn by the private sector in rail" and will enable "more than 6400 extra services each week by 2021, benefitting all parts of the country."

Cheap finance and government encouragement to include new trains in franchise bids has led to something of a 'bubble' in the last three years, creating huge demand for new vehicles. However, it is also creating problems for train-builders, Rolling Stock Owning Companies (ROSCOs) and

porterbrook

operators. What will happen to the factories and production lines when the 'bubble' bursts? And what will happen to the thousands of perfectly serviceable trains from the 1980s, 1990s and 2000s rendered redundant before their time by a combination of new trains and the abandonment of the rolling nationwide electrification programme?

To find out more about this phenomenon, and how one rolling stock owner is reacting to a rapidly changing market, I spoke to Porterbrook's chief commercial officer, Stephen McGurk.

COMMUNICATING BENEFITS
WHAT ROLE DOES PORTERBROOK PLAY IN THE INDUSTRY AS A ROLLING STOCK OWNER?

"We do much more than just lease trains. We ensure that passenger rolling stock meets the needs of our clients and their passengers, we support British engineering through refurbishment programmes and projects such as Class 769 'Flex' (see page 88). Our focus on engineering has allowed us to develop a deep expertise but also to optimise the performance of the stock."

Stephen continues: "As well as investing in new trains, we finance the refurbishment and upgrading of existing stock to modern standards and have already invested more than £300 million in this process. As a result, enhanced passenger comfort and safety creates the effect of new trains, thereby extending the operational life of the vehicles.

"With that expertise and innovation we can also take off-lease vehicles and re-purpose them for new operators and different roles. We like to think Porterbrook is at the forefront of that movement.

"The 'Flex' project is evidence of what we can do as an asset manager. Since receiving the original order for eight trains from Arriva Rail North, we've sold more to Arriva Trains Wales and the 19 Great Western Railway sets will be like new trains, complete with air-cooling and upgraded interiors.

"Another advantage of re-using existing trains is that they aren't subject to the 'teething troubles' experienced by every fleet of new trains. They have good MTIN (Miles per Technical Incident Number) figures as maintenance teams and their owners have extensive experience of their performance and have often invested in replacing unreliable components to improve them."

In recent years, there's been a move away

from the practice of financing new rolling stock through one of the three original ROSCOs formed during the privatisation process in the mid-1990s. Why are operators turning to these international financial institutions instead of railway specialists?

"In the past, ROSCOs haven't explained their role in asset management and the value we add through our long-term maintenance and improvement programmes. We became complacent," adds Stephen, bluntly.

"We haven't properly communicated the benefits we offer. For example, the fleets owned and supported by Porterbrook have won more than 50% of the 'Golden Spanner' prizes ever awarded [for reliability]. We really value engineering – in fact, more than half of our 120 employees are engineers."

CHALLENGING
HOW DOES STEPHEN VIEW THE CURRENT MARKET FOR RAIL VEHICLES IN THE UK?

"It's astonishing," he says. "There are 7000 vehicles on order or being delivered – it's never been done before and it's hugely challenging. A large number of those new trains rely on the same supply chain and what will happen if that is disrupted?

"We are facing an unprecedented volume of new trains over the next few years. Not only have the train-builders never delivered such high numbers of vehicles in such a short space of time; operators and infrastructure managers have never been asked to approve so many new trains for service at the same time. And many of them are new designs that will require a more extensive approvals process before they can enter service. They will inevitably take time to bed in, and this will affect performance over the coming years.

"As an industry, we always complain about the 'boom and bust' cycle of train orders. We're in a 'boom' period again and it's not sustainable for anyone.

"Porterbrook is here to support train operators in whatever way we can, but we also need to champion our aftermarket companies and a supply chain that supports thousands of engineering jobs across the country. We will spend approximately £130m with 100 UK-based companies throughout 2018. At the moment, the focus is on PRM-TSI accessibility modifications and the aftermarket companies are extremely busy. But what will happen

when that work dries up after January 1, 2020?"

A recent Porterbrook supply chain consultation, surveying companies with a total UK turnover of £1.87bn and 6900 employees, concluded that a minimum 30% reduction in the number of refurbished fleets in the market in 2019 would lead to a 12% decrease in industry turnover to £1.64bn and a 7% cut in employment, from 6900 to 6400 jobs. It also reported that following a minimum 30% reduction in the number of refurbished fleets in the market, in 2022 there would be an 8% decrease in turnover and a further 8% decrease in employment levels (to 6300) from current levels.

Refurbishment turnover and employment are expected to fall from 2019, with component suppliers and service providers the worst affected. While new-build turnover and employment levels are predicted to increase in 2019 through to 2022 as new fleets are constructed, that sector is much smaller than the refurbishment sub-sector, so the increase is unlikely to offset any decreases in aftermarket employment. Long-term, this will have a detrimental effect on the UK supply chain and aftermarket refurbishment specialists, with engineering and manufacturing jobs likely to be lost, or switched to other sectors.

Many in the supply chain also believe that due to the limited number of UK train manufacturers, the industry will become increasingly dependent on international imports, and it will become less competitive and more expensive. Similarly, many believe that a shortage of engineers is limiting UK innovation and expertise.

"Unfortunately, if we continue on the current path," says Stephen, "it will become difficult to obtain a good quality existing train, as they won't be available and the supply chain's ability to provide a quality refurbishment will have diminished."

What can Porterbrook and the other rolling stock owners do to smooth out the peaks and troughs in train-building and refurbishment?

"The message we want to get out is that Porterbrook is not a 'flash in the pan'. We're here for the long-term to support new and old. Trains are a long-term investment.

"Porterbrook's culture is of being highly proactive and pioneering, as evidenced by the purchase of the first new passenger trains in the UK post-privatisation and the subsequent award of the largest single order of new vehicles with the purchase of 700 Class 377 'Electrostar' vehicles. To date, Porterbrook has invested in 2300 new

porterbrook

Left: Porterbrook supports train operators and aftermarket suppliers and train refurbishment companies through contracts for improvements to the existing fleet. A £1m contract was recently awarded for the installation of wheelslide protection (WSP) equipment to Porterbrook Class 153s operating with Greater Anglia, East Midlands Trains and West Midlands Railway. On August 18, 2016 a GA Class 153 crosses Oulton Broad Swing Bridge with the 1207 Lowestoft-Ipswich. ROBIN STEWART-SMITH

Right: Over the last two decades, Porterbrook has invested in more than 2300 new vehicles for British operators, including a massive order for 700 Bombardier 'Electrostar' vehicles. Southern's No. 377130 arrives at Lewes on July 11, 2016. Some of these trains could eventually be converted to bi-mode operation to help eliminate diesel trains from the Southern fleet. CHRISTOPHER J WILSON

passenger vehicles for the UK rail industry. We are starting to see some hopeful signs that the Government's attitude to older trains is changing. There's a recognition in the next East Midlands franchise Invitation to Tender (ITT) document that trains can be existing or new, which is helpful."

INNOVATION

HOW DOES PORTERBROOK PLAN TO SQUARE ITS COMMITMENT TO OLDER FLEETS WITH THE DEPARTMENT FOR TRANSPORT'S ASPIRATION TO ELIMINATE DIESEL-POWERED TRAINS FROM THE NETWORK BY 2040?

"The Secretary of State for Transport and his rail minister challenged the industry earlier this year to find viable alternatives to diesel traction. Porterbrook is already doing that – we're looking at the possibilities offered by batteries, hydrogen and bi-mode trains.

"We're also working closely with the UK Rail Research and Innovation Network (UKRRIN) to see if we can develop something locally

in the UK more quickly than we could by working with big international suppliers.

"Our plan is to develop an 'Innovation Train' using an off-lease Class 319. We're encouraging UK suppliers to install their innovative technology on our train and have it tested in the real world. By working together we can quickly develop new technologies, make them more reliable and bring production costs down to benefit everyone. Porterbrook recently announced that it is committed to investing £1bn in UK rail over the next five years. Our recent refinancing package has put us in the best possible position to do that. Our doors are open!

"We're also looking at the potential of 'Flex' trains for freight and parcels operations. We're working with [transport consultancy] Intermodality and the big supermarkets on proposals for a 'go anywhere' train capable of carrying parcels and lightweight freight at up to 100mph. To test the principle, a prototype train with seats removed and racking installed will deliver Christmas presents donated by the supermarkets to children in Great Ormond Street Hospital this December – it's an exciting prospect and we hope to build on this if the appetite is there.

"Also being investigated is a train with passenger seats that can be folded away to create space for parcels, luggage, cycles or sports equipment. In theory, it could be used during the day as a 'crowd-buster' on busy passenger routes and for freight traffic overnight."

What about other EMU fleets, such as the SWR Class 455s and London Northwestern Railway

Class 350/2s, which represent major investments by Porterbrook, but will soon be surplus to requirements?

"We still believe that there's a role for train fleets displaced from the likes of Greater Anglia, South Western Railway and West Midlands. There is a range of opportunities for the '455s' in their traditional operating area, but we have some very interesting and innovative early proposals for self-powered options too.

"The Class 350/2s are our highest profile displaced trains. But as the UK's most reliable passenger train fleet over the last few years, they should also find new homes once they are released by West Midlands Railway. We're exploring options to release them to new operators such as Thameslink Southern Great Northern (TSGN), East Midlands Railway for the new Corby service from 2019 and new operators on the West Coast Main Line. They're a flexible and capable train and the interiors can be reconfigured for a variety of roles, from metro to long-distance work."

"Our new chief executive officer, Mary Grant, comes from an operations background and she ensures that every one of us is acutely aware of the needs of train operating companies. We must always be thinking of what they need and how we can best help to deliver it."

Below: Two Porterbrook fleets already displaced by new trains and being redeployed are the Thameslink Class 319s and 377/5s. On September 5, 2011 Nos. 319439 and 377521 stop to change voltage at Farringdon in central London while forming Thameslink services from Bedford to Brighton and vice versa. While the '377s' are now operating alongside other 'Electrostars' for Southern, the '319s' are finding a variety of new roles and Porterbrook is examining various possibilities for the class. BRIAN MORRISON

porterbrook

porterbrook

PEOPLE MOVERS

A growing urban population requires good public transport to keep cities moving efficiently. Expensive enhancements to the existing network and new railways such as Crossrail require a new generation of high-capacity trains built to shift large numbers of people quickly and reliably.

Having assumed responsibility for many of London's inner-suburban and orbital routes, London Overground is investing in new trains to increase capacity and frequencies. This Class 710 'Aventra' EMU is one of 54 on order from Bombardier for the Gospel Oak-Barking, North London, West London and Liverpool Street-Enfield/Chingford/Cheshunt routes. BEN JONES

porterbrook

Thameslink Class 700

First mooted in the 1990s, this £7 billion project to provide more frequent trains to more destinations and better north-south links across London has had its fair share of challenges, not least with the trains that were built to operate the intensive service.

Making use of former goods tunnels underneath central London, the Thameslink operation has its origins with BR and Network SouthEast in the late-1980s. It provided new links between the Midland Main Line south of Bedford and various destinations on the Southern Region, including Gatwick Airport and Brighton.

In many ways a victim of its own success, planning for a major expansion of the service – billed as Thameslink 2000 – started a few years after the operation was launched in 1988. However, privatisation in the mid-1990s, the collapse of Railtrack in 2001 and priorities elsewhere on the network meant that it was not until the late-2000s that work began in earnest to expand Thameslink.

In 2011, the consortium Cross London Trains (XLT), consisting of Siemens, venture capitalists 3i Infrastructure and Innisfree, was announced as the preferred bidder for the £1.6bn deal to build and maintain the huge new fleet of trains. The decision was politically controversial as the trains were to be built at Krefeld in Germany, rather than in the UK, as promised by Bombardier. Both the procurement process and final close of contract were delayed, resulting in the first delivery date moving back from 2012 to 2016. Despite the procurement process starting as long ago as 2008, the final contract was not signed until June 2013. Around the same time, Eversholt Rail Leasing was appointed as the asset manager for the Class 700 fleet.

Bidders were expected to provide not just the trains, but also depots for maintenance and stabling, and finance for the rolling stock project, generating revenue from the long-term leasing of rolling stock to the Train Operating Company (TOC) and associated maintenance payments.

The Department for Transport's (DfT) specification included: high reliability, short station dwell times, integrated information technology including passenger information and information for vehicle maintenance, a maximum speed of 100mph and high acceleration and deceleration performance to cater for the planned high-frequency timetable.

The DfT also asked for the trains to be lighter than existing EMUs, exerting lower track forces and demonstrating high energy efficiency. A standard 12-car train was to be approximately 240m (790ft) long and an eight-car set around 160m (530ft).

Consortiums led by Alstom, Bombardier, Hitachi Rail Europe and Siemens were shortlisted for the deal in July 2008, although Hitachi dropped out the following year. Siemens' offer was the new 'Desiro City' EMU, a development of the technology employed in its successful and reliable Desiro UK family and the Desiro Mainline EMU, built for use in Germany, Belgium and Austria. Bombardier offered its new 'Aventra' design, developed from the hugely successful 'Electrostar' and Alstom's pitch centred around the novel 'X'trapolis UK', an articulated design with just one bogie supporting each of the short cars.

fleet of Bombardier-built Class 377 'Electrostars' that were introduced in the late-2000s.

The first set, No. 700108, entered passenger service on June 20, 2016 and over the following year they took over all Govia Thameslink Railway (GTR) services, allowing the older trains to be cascaded elsewhere. However, deliveries continued into 2018, with the fleet building up in preparation for the new, more intensive timetable planned for May 2018.

Originally expected to feature 24 trains per hour (tph) through the 'core' tunnels between St Pancras International and Blackfriars, using Automatic Train Operation (ATO) to provide additional capacity and reliability, the introduction of the full timetable has been put back to December 2019 to allow more time for the trains and new signalling technology to bed in. Unfortunately,

> "The trains are just one part of a huge enhancement programme undertaken across London and the south east of England over the last few years, including the £1bn reconstruction of London Bridge station.

ENHANCEMENT

The trains are just one part of a huge enhancement project undertaken across London and the south-east of England over the last few years. Work has included the £1bn reconstruction of London Bridge station, the total redesign and extension of Blackfriars station, the construction of new junctions, tunnels and grade-separated junctions at various locations, extra tracks, platform extensions and new signalling to accommodate the extra trains. Two new depots, costing £150 million, have also been built, at Three Bridges in Surrey and Hornsey in north London to maintain the fleet, along with new and upgraded stabling and servicing facilities at several locations, including Peterborough and Bedford.

A fleet of 60 eight-car (Class 700/0) and 55 12-car trains (Class 700/1) entered service between Spring 2016 and June 2018, replacing Thameslink's ex-BR Class 319s and a smaller

even the initial offering of 18tph from May 20, 2018 proved impossible to deliver, resulting in delays, overcrowding and anger from GTR passengers who had been promised a 'step change' in services.

Eventually, Thameslink will provide frequent links between Bedford, Luton, Cambridge and Peterborough north of the Thames with Gatwick, Brighton, Orpington, Sutton, Rainham and Maidstone in the south, including a direct interchange with east-west Crossrail services at Farringdon.

CONTROVERSIAL

As hinted above, the Class 700s have proved controversial since the contract was first awarded to Siemens, and this has continued since their first contact with the travelling public.

The Government-specified trains have been widely criticised for their spartan interiors, uncomfortable seats, lack of free wi-fi and

porterbrook

SIEMENS CLASS 700 'DESIRO CITY'

Operator: Thameslink
Supplier: Siemens, Krefeld
Built: 2015-18
Order Value: £1.6bn
Owner/finance: Cross London Trains
Introduced: June 2016-June 2018
No. ordered: 115 (1140 vehicles)
No. of cars per train: Eight (700/0), 12 (700/1)
Numbers: 700001-060, 700101-155
Formation: DMCO-PTSO-MSO-TSO-TSO-MSO-PTSO-DMCO (700/0), DMCO-PTSO-MSO-MSO-TSO-TSO-TSO-TSO-MSO-MSO-PTSO-DMCO (700/1)
Power supply: 25kv AC overhead and 750v DC third-rail
Max speed: 100mph
Power rating: 4400hp (Class 700/0), 6700hp (700/1)
Capacity: Class 700/0 - 427 seats (52 First/373 Standard), 719 standing. Class 700/1 - 666 seats (52 First/614 Standard), 1088 standing.
Weight: 278 tonnes (700/0), 410 tonnes (700/1)
Features: Air-conditioning, longitudinal metro-style seating, wide gangways within set, fast-acting sliding doors, wi-fi (from 2018), passenger information systems
Routes: Peterborough/Cambridge/Bedford-London-Brighton/Horsham/Maidstone/Littlehampton

A major part of the Thameslink Programme was the £1bn rebuilding of London Bridge station, completed in January 2018. On June 1, eight-car Class 700/0 No. 700040 pauses with a southbound service. BEN JONES

700040

porterbrook

Left: The powered version of the lightweight Siemens SF7000 bogie with inside frames, designed to be at least 30% lighter than the SF5000 bogie used on older Siemens trains for the UK market. BEN JONES

Below: The DfT-specified interiors of the Class 700s have been the subject of fierce criticism from Thameslink passengers, with uncomfortable seats, a lack of tables and wi-fi and fewer seats than the trains they replaced. BEN JONES

power sockets, heating and ventilation problems, not to mention the 'teething troubles' associated with any new train design.

At the time of their construction, passenger numbers were rising rapidly and with London's population continuing to grow, the emphasis was on providing the maximum capacity possible – especially for standing passengers. However, Thameslink serves many different markets, from commuters to leisure traffic, travellers with heavy luggage to and from Gatwick and Luton airports and short-distance metro flows across the capital.

Seating is based around a 2+2 arrangement, with fold-up seats and large areas around the doors for standing passengers. No tables are provided in the bays of four seats, and no flip-down tables are fitted in the 'airline' style seats, causing further criticism from regular users.

The 12-car trains have First Class accommodation in the driving cars, but otherwise all seating is Standard Class.

One of the major criticisms of the Class 700s has been the seating. A 12-car set has 666 seats, compared to 714 on a 12-car Class 377/5 or 807 on a 12-car Great Northern Class 365 EMU. Fewer seats means more room for standing passengers, and greater capacity overall, but Thameslink routes carry large numbers of long-distance commuters with journey times well over an hour in many cases. Many passengers on the Thameslink route have also criticised the firmness and width of the seats, which have been likened to ironing boards. GTR and the DfT have defended the '700' seats, saying that they are designed to meet current fire safety regulations and, in one instance, that the seats 'would become softer with regular use'.

WORLD FIRST

The trains are designed for Driver Only Operation (DOO) and features include GSM-R communications radio, as well as standard Automatic Warning

System (AWS), Train Protection Warning System (TPWS) and, in a world-first, Automatic Train Operation (ATO) equipment laid over European Train Control System (ETCS) Level 2 safety systems. ATO was specified to provide the necessary additional capacity in the core tunnels.

Like their predecessors, the Class 700s are built to operate on 750v DC third-rail and 25kv AC overhead electrification systems, the changeover point being Farringdon in both directions. Other features include regenerative braking, modular components to reduce 'down time' at depot visits, remote diagnostics that allow the train to report faults back to the depot and give engineers the option of interrogating train management systems remotely to check for any issues.

Each eight-car Class 700/1 has four powered cars and four trailers, marshalled as two (almost) identical four-car half-sets. Each half has a Driving Motor Composite (DMCO) containing the driving cab and First Class saloon, Pantograph Trailer Standard Open (PTSO), Motor Standard Open (MSO) and a Trailer Standard Open (TSO). Of the two TSOs coupled in the centre of the set, one is fitted with an accessible toilet.

The 12-car trains feature a similar formation, with the DMCO and PTSO vehicles at the outer ends, but they have two MSOs and an additional TSO vehicle per half-train, although there is still only one toilet per train. Full-width gangways are fitted between cars within the set, providing better access right through the train and improving security and safety for passengers, especially at night.

The motor cars have one Siemens 200kW asynchronous traction motor on each of their four axles, with an IGBT inverter control system.

Like many new generation passenger vehicles the Class 700s are mounted on lightweight inside-framed bogies to save weight. In this case,

the bogie is the Siemens SF7000, designed and built in Austria for the UK market. Development of the new bogie type began in 2007 in response to feedback gained from use of the SF5000 bogie on earlier Siemens trains in the UK. The new bogie was designed to reduce energy consumption and track access charges and weight-saving elements included a shorter wheelbase, inside frames, a bolster-less design and hollow axles. The first prototypes were completed in 2011.

Total weight is 6.3 tonnes (powered) and 4.4 tonnes (unpowered), a reduction of around 30% over the SF5000 design. At the time, the decision to procure a train with an all-new,

porterbrook

untested bogie design was seen as a risk, especially as Bombardier already had a proven low-weight bogie developed in the UK.

The primary suspension system uses layered rubber, with pneumatic secondary suspension. The motor bogie wheelbase is 2200mm with 820mm diameter wheels. There are tread brakes and two axle-mounted disc brakes per axle on trailer bogies and the power bogies feature regenerative braking.

Assembly of the pre-series Class 700s began before the formal financial close of the project in mid-2013. Testing of a 12-car set began at Siemens' Wegberg-Wildenrath Test and Validation Centre in Germany in March 2014. Part of set No. 700001 was displayed to the public at the InnoTrans trade fair in Berlin in September 2014.

The first completed train arrived in the UK towards the end of July 2015, and was delivered direct to the new Three Bridges depot. It made its first test runs on the Brighton Main Line in December of that year.

The first train in public service was No. 700108, which worked the 10.02 Brighton-London Bridge on June 20, 2016. All 115 sets were delivered by rail to the UK, running via Belgium, France and the Channel Tunnel. GB Railfreight handled the delivery runs on the UK side, with later sets towed north to Peterborough before running round and working back south to Hornsey for acceptance.

Having taken over the full Thameslink service from Class 319s and Class 377s by autumn 2017, the class started to appear on Great Northern services from February 2018, including 'preview' services running from Brighton to Cambridge and Peterborough via the new Canal Tunnel link.

The final 12-car set, No. 700146, was delivered by rail to the UK on May 23, 2018, with Nos. 700059/060 completing the eight-car fleet the following month.

While their introduction has been controversial at times and the massive Thameslink system upgrade will need some time to bed in, once everything is in place the Class 700s will play a significant role in increasing capacity for commuters into and across London. The expanded network will add 80 more stations to the Thameslink network, creating many new journey opportunities and adding space for up to 60,000 extra peak time passengers by 2019.

CLASS 345:

LONDON'S NEW EAST-WEST CONGESTION BUSTER

The £15 billion Crossrail project is finally coming to fruition after years of disruptive construction work. When its new Bombardier-built trains start to run under central London in December they are expected to revolutionise travel across the capital.

While Thameslink is designed to provide better north-south connections across London, the new £14.8bn Crossrail route runs east to west, linking Shenfield, Abbey Wood and Canary Wharf with Heathrow Airport and the Thames Valley via the City of London and the West End. It's a remarkable achievement that was, at one point, Europe's largest construction project. It's also another major rail project that has taken more than two decades to come to fruition.

New tunnels under central London will be phased into use from December 2018, introducing a high frequency metro operation using 70 nine-car Class 345 'Aventra' EMUs built by Bombardier in Derby.

Those 'Aventras' are already in limited service with TfL Rail in east London, accumulating miles and gaining useful service experience on the Liverpool Street-Shenfield route. Since May 20, they've also started work in the west of the capital, with two sets per day diagrammed on Paddington-Hayes & Harlington all-station services alongside ex-Heathrow Connect Class 360s. With infrastructure improvements still ongoing, the interim services are worked by seven-car trains, but the standard '345' formation will be nine cars, capable of transporting up to 1500 passengers rapidly across the capital.

From December 2018, the next piece of the Crossrail jigsaw will be in place, as the Class 345s start to run through the central London tunnels, linking Abbey Wood with Paddington. In December 2019, the full 'Elizabeth line' service is expected to start, transforming connections across London with up to 24 trains per hour (tph) in each direction, linking Shenfield, Abbey Wood and Canary Wharf in the east with Heathrow Airport, Maidenhead and Reading in the west.

Crossrail will bring much-needed extra capacity for a growing 'world city' desperate for better mobility. It will boost central London's rail capacity by 10% at a stroke, while also supporting regeneration east and west of the capital, and drastically reduce journey times across the city. Around 200 million people are expected to use Crossrail services each year when it is completed.

porterbrook

BOMBARDIER CLASS 345 'AVENTRA'

Operator:	Transport for London
Owner/finance:	Transport for London
Built:	2015-18
Introduced:	Phased from mid-2017, full service from December 2019
No. ordered:	70 (originally 66, with options for 20 more)
No. of cars per train:	Nine (total 630 vehicles)
Numbers:	345001-070
Order value:	£1bn
Routes:	Shenfield/Abbey Wood to Heathrow/Reading via Crossrail tunnels
Power supply:	25kv AC overhead
Max speed:	90mph
Power rating:	20x Bombardier 250kW traction motors per train (5mW)
Formation:	DMSO(A)+ PMSO(A)+ MSO(A)+ MSO(B)+ TSO+MSO(C)+ MSO(D)+PMSO(B)+ DMSOB)
Capacity:	454 seats
Features:	Air-conditioning, longitudinal metro-style seating, wide gangways within set, sliding plug doors

Testing of the new railway is well underway, with Class 345s gradually running deeper into the tunnels under central London. In April, No. 345025 passes Custom House (close to the ExCeL exhibition centre in east London) with a test run from Abbey Wood.
CROSSRAIL

Top: Taylor Woodrow completed the £142m depot at Old Oak Common for the Crossrail fleet in early-2018. It will be the main base for the fleet of 70 trains, although stabling and servicing will take place at several other locations.
CROSSRAIL

Above: Since May 2018, a small fleet of seven-car '345s' has been working TfL Rail inner-suburban services between Paddington and Hayes & Harlington. Once the full Crossrail service is launched, the trains will not normally be seen at Paddington's high-level platforms.
BEN JONES

Crossrail will bring an extra 1.5m people within 45 minutes of central London, link the city's key employment, leisure and business districts, including Heathrow, the West End, the City of London and Docklands, promising benefits of up to £42bn for the UK's economy.

REGIONAL METRO

Ordered by Transport for London (TfL) in February 2014, the 200m-long Class 345 trains were first revealed in late 2015 and are the result of close co-operation between Bombardier and its client.

From December 2019, the Crossrail network will be more than 62 miles (100km) long, stretching from Reading and Heathrow Airport in the west to Shenfield in Essex and Abbey Wood in north Kent.

While the core section is an entirely new railway, more than £1bn is also being invested by Network Rail to upgrade the Great Western and Great Eastern lines at each end. Work includes the renewal and upgrading of track, power supply equipment and signalling, platform extensions to accommodate the new trains and the rebuilding of numerous stations to increase capacity, ready for the introduction of the new services.

Mark Wild, TfL's managing director for London Underground and the Elizabeth line, said: "The opening of the Elizabeth line in December will redefine transport in London with journeys made easier and trains passing through brand new tunnels beneath central London to new, accessible stations. The additional trains will allow us to serve all the terminals at Heathrow and provide an increased frequency when the line is fully open in December 2019."

Nine years after the Crossrail construction work began, No. 345021 was the first of its class to run under its own power into the new tunnels on February 25/26, when it worked a 5.5km test from Abbey Wood to Connaught Tunnel. It was the first of hundreds of test runs, gradually probing deeper into the tunnels at increasing speeds to test the integrity of signalling, infrastructure and safety systems. By the summer of 2018, Crossrail was hoping to able to operate a 'shadow' service of 24tph over the new route, ready for the introduction of Phase 3 (Paddington Low Level-Abbey Wood) service in December.

May 2019 will see that service expanded with the introduction of Paddington (Low Level) to Shenfield trains in Phase 4, followed by the full service in December 2019.

The first Class 345s to enter passenger service were filtered into Liverpool Street-Shenfield diagrams by TfL Rail in the summer of 2017, temporarily shortened to seven cars due to the shorter platforms at Liverpool Street. All 70 trains will be running as nine-car sets by the end of 2019.

From May 2018, a small number of seven-car Class 345s were introduced on Paddington-Hayes & Harlington stopping services, working alongside ex-Heathrow Connect Class 360/2s. Phase 2 should have seen the '345s' working into Heathrow Airport, but issues with their ETCS signalling systems on the privately-owned airport branch prevented this happening as planned.

MADE IN BRITAIN

The Class 345s are being constructed by Bombardier Transportation at its Litchurch Lane plant in Derby. The initial order for 65 sets was increased to 66 when it was confirmed that the Crossrail service would be extended to Reading. Since then, another four sets have been added at a cost of £73 million, taking the total fleet to 70 nine-car trains.

Bombardier's contract has benefits far beyond London and Derby, directly supporting 760 jobs and 80 apprenticeships, plus 55,000 further UK jobs throughout the supply chain. Around 2000 people are employed by Bombardier in Derby, 800 of whom are directly engaged in building 'Aventra' vehicles.

Over the last decade, the £14.8bn Crossrail tunnels have been Europe's largest construction project, employing thousands of engineers and contractors. They will see their first Class 345s carrying passengers in December. CROSSRAIL

Peter Doolin, Bombardier Transportation's vice president projects, Crossrail & London Underground, said: "The Crossrail trains are based on our very latest Aventra product platform, which we're proud to say has been designed and developed as a technology leading train for the UK."

Initially, the first few trains were tested at Litchurch Lane before being moved to Old Dalby for high-speed dynamic testing and then dispatched to Ilford for further tests. Later deliveries are being made directly to Ilford and Old Oak Common and at least one set underwent extensive testing on the West Coast Main Line from Crewe in 2017/18.

Each train can carry up to 1500 passengers and features air-conditioning, interconnecting walk-through carriages, and they have been designed with an emphasis on energy-efficiency and intelligent on-train energy management systems. The trains also incorporate technologically advanced condition-based maintenance systems, including Bombardier's Orbita predictive maintenance

and Automated Vehicle Inspection system.

To help deliver the planned service frequency of 24tph, the Class 345s are fitted with Automatic Train Operation (ATO) and European Train Control System (ETCS) equipment, which will take control of the trains in the core tunnels. ATO increases capacity on metro-style lines by allowing trains to run closer together – known as shorter headways – more safely and, in theory, delivering shorter, more consistent dwell times at stations.

ATO is also necessary to ensure the trains stop exactly where they should at stations in the core tunnels, which are all fitted with platform-edge screens and doors to increase passenger safety and comfort.

CHALLENGE

At just over 200m in length, the Class 345s are more than 50% longer than the longest London Underground train or 18 of the modern 'Routemaster' buses. However, Bombardier was challenged to keep their weight down and

porterbrook

Above: Class 345s are unusual in having three sets of double doors per car, allowing passengers to board and alight rapidly, reducing dwell times at stations. BEN JONES

Below left: A Class 345 intermediate car on the Derby assembly line receiving underfloor equipment prior to being lowered onto its bogies for the first time. BEN JONES

Below right: Completed Class 345s in the recently-built test house at Bombardier's Litchurch Lane factory in Derby on June 28. BEN JONES

deliver high energy efficiency, but still offer quick acceleration and good levels of passenger comfort.

Lighting levels and heating and air-conditioning are automatically controlled to suit ambient conditions and regenerative braking will feed electricity back into overhead lines during braking, saving up to 30% energy.

Like the Thameslink Class 700s, large areas around the doors allow faster boarding and alighting and additional room for standing passengers. A mix of longitudinal metro-style (as seen on London Overground's Class 378s) and a limited number of seating bays is available throughout the train, much like London Underground's 'S8' trains used on Metropolitan Line services.

TfL reports that the interior design and colour palette "has been carefully selected to provide an accessible and welcoming environment. The design includes darker floors and natural finish materials that will wear in and not wear out, ensuring they retain their high-quality feel for years to come."

It adds: "The light-coloured ceilings also maximise the feeling of height and openness inside the new trains. The material and colour choices also align with Crossrail stations for a consistent customer experience."

On-train passenger information systems deliver real-time travel information, enabling passengers to plan onward journeys while on board. Free wi-fi is available on trains and platforms, and passengers will have access to 4G mobile networks, even in the long tunnels under London.

As with all new trains, the '345s' are fully accessible, with four dedicated wheelchair spaces per nine-car set. There are also multi-purpose spaces with tip-up seats where pushchairs, bikes and bulky luggage can be stowed.

Howard Smith, TfL's operations director of Crossrail, says: "The trains will have walk-through carriages, each with three wide doorways per car to enable people to get on and off quickly. They will have air-conditioning and use the latest technology to provide customers with real-time travel information

to help them plan their onward journeys."

Bombardier has invested hugely in its 'Aventra' programme, including the construction of an all-new assembly hall and test facility at its Derby site, the benefits of which will extend to other 'Aventra' orders for London Overground, South Western Railway, Greater Anglia and others.

An impressive depot facility, costing £142m, has been built by Taylor Woodrow at Old Oak Common to act as a 'mothership' for the new fleet. Servicing is also being undertaken, initially at Ilford, where Bombardier already has a presence. New and upgraded stabling facilities have also been provided at Shenfield, Gidea Park and Maidenhead.

The Class 345 'Aventra' for Crossrail is the first of Bombardier's new generation of EMUs and marks a significant evolution over the previous 'Electrostar' family. 'Aventra' is the culmination of consultation and evaluation held over a number of years, taking the best elements of 'Electrostar' to offer a heavily standardised train platform that can be adapted to suit specific operator and passenger requirements.

porterbrook

MODERN TRAINS
FOR MOORGATE

Linking Hertfordshire and Cambridgeshire with the City of London, Great Northern's inner-suburban services are currently worked by some of the oldest passenger trains on the network – but not for much longer.

All 25 Class 717s are being tested at Siemens' Wildenrath test centre in western Germany prior to delivery by rail to the UK. GARY BOYD-HOPE

If these trains look vaguely familiar, there's a very good reason. Great Northern's new Class 717s are a close relative of the Thameslink Class 700s, adapted for use in the old 'widened lines' tunnels that link the East Coast Main Line to Moorgate, right in the heart of the City of London.

In 1976 these services were transformed by electrification and commuters swapped outdated 1950s Mk 1 compartment stock and diesel units that were unsuited to the long tunnels, for bright, modern Class 313 inner-suburban EMUs. Restricted clearances in the tunnels between Drayton Park and Moorgate meant that electrification at 25kv AC overhead wasn't possible, so 750v DC third-rail was adopted, necessitating the use of dual-voltage trains. That legacy continues today, although dual voltage trains are more common than they were in 1976. The Class 313s continue to work the Moorgate route more than 40 years after their debut, making them the oldest electric units still in regular service in the UK. While they have given loyal service,

both on the Great Northern and elsewhere, they are showing their age and authority was given to replace them in 2015. Passenger numbers have doubled on the Moorgate line in the last 15 years, so increased capacity was vital, although the restricted length of the platforms between Drayton Park and Moorgate precluded the option of longer trains.

Govia Thameslink Railway (GTR), which holds the massive and complex Thameslink Southern Great Northern (TSGN) management contract, opted for a six-car variant of the Siemens 'Desiro City', 115

porterbrook

SIEMENS CLASS 717

Operator:	Great Northern
Supplier:	Siemens, Krefeld
Built:	2017/18
Introduced:	December 2018
No. ordered:	25 (150 vehicles)
No. of cars per train:	Six
Numbers:	717001-025
Order value:	£200 million
Routes:	Moorgate-Hertford North/ Welwyn-Royston
Power supply:	25kv AC overhead and 750v DC third-rail
Max speed:	85mph
Power rating:	TBC
Formation:	DMSO+TSO+TSO+ MSO+ PTSO+DMSO
Capacity:	362 seats, 581 standing
Features:	Air-conditioning, rapid deployment emergency steps at each cab end, wide gangways within set, fast-acting sliding doors, wi-fi, passenger information systems
Owner/finance:	Rock Rail Moorgate

Above: No. 717001 on test at Wildenrath on March 10. The trains will be delivered by rail via the Channel Tunnel to Hornsey depot during the second half of the year. STEFAN GEERTSEN

Inset: Class 717 passenger saloon, showing the similarities with Thameslink's Class 700s - including the unpopular 'ironing board' seats. GARY BOYD-HOPE

Above: A key feature for operation in the restricted Moorgate tunnels are the emergency egress steps built into the cabs of each train. These can be deployed very quickly in the event of an emergency. GARY BOYD-HOPE

of which were already on order for Thameslink.

In December 2015, GTR announced that it had selected Siemens to build 25 trains as a follow-on order from the Thameslink Class 700 order. The order was finalised in February 2016 and construction started the following year at Siemens' Krefeld factory in western Germany. Unlike the Class 313s, which run singly as three-car or in pairs as six-car formations, the '717s' are fixed formation trains built to the maximum length possible on the Moorgate line. They are intended to increase peak time capacity on the busy commuter route and will also be used to deliver

a higher frequency timetable between Moorgate, Hertford North, Stevenage and Royston in 2019. The first set is due to be introduced in August, with all 25 in use by spring 2019. The first sets arrived in the UK in June to start main line testing.

GTR's choice of Siemens for this order is based upon the logical decision to standardise, as much as possible, the trains used on the Great Northern route. In terms of equipment and passenger accommodation, the '717s' are very close to the Class 700s now working longer distance Thameslink routes to Peterborough and Cambridge. It should also prove quicker and easier to train staff who are already familiar with the design on the '717s' when they arrive at Hornsey depot in north London. GTR staff will maintain the fleet, with support from Siemens.

EVACUATION DOORS

A significant difference between Class 717s and the earlier Class 700s is the provision of emergency evacuation doors in the centre of the cab ends. These are mandatory for operation in the Moorgate tunnels, which don't have evacuation platforms along the tunnel walls, like many modern underground railways.

Unlike the Class 313s, which rely on passengers descending a wooden ladder from a conventional door next to the driving cab, the '717s' feature fast-acting folding steps, which deploy from their housing in just a few seconds to give passengers a much safer (and quicker) route out of the train in the event of an emergency in the tunnels.

Otherwise, the trains are very similar to their Class 700 cousins, featuring a bright - if somewhat spartan - interior, with a mix of airline seats and bays of four arranged in 2+2 format. They also have fold-up seats and large areas around the doors for standing passengers. No First Class accommodation or toilets are provided.

The cars are 20.2m (66ft) long and 2.8m (9ft 2in) wide with full width gangways allowing easy passage through the train, increasing capacity and

safety for passengers, especially at night. Other features include Liebherr intelligent climate control and air-conditioning and wi-fi. Unusually, the sliding pocket doors have two settings – a rapid mode for inner-city stations to reduce dwell times, and a slower setting for stations outside the busiest sections.

Each set has three powered cars and three trailers. The trains are designed for Driver Only Operation (DOO) and features include GSM-R communications radio, as well standard Automatic Warning System (AWS), Train Protection Warning System (TPWS) and provision for the installation of European Train Control System (ETCS) Level 2 cab signalling. GTR hopes to install this before the end of its management contract, but it is not currently clear when Network Rail will introduce ETCS on the Great Northern route – it is, however, one of the priorities for NR's 'Digital Railway' programme.

Like their predecessors, the Class 717s are built to operate on 750v DC third-rail and 25kv AC overhead electrification systems, the changeover point being Drayton Park in both directions. Other features include regenerative braking, modular components to reduce 'downtime' at depot visits, remote diagnostics that allow the train to report faults back to the depot and give engineers the option of interrogating train management systems remotely to check for any issues.

The motor cars have four Siemens 200kW asynchronous traction motors (one on each axle) with an IGBT inverter control system.

The Class 717s are also mounted on Siemens' lightweight SF7000 inside-framed bogies to save weight.

Great Northern's initial plan is for the Class 717s to work 21 diagrams in existing schedules, although it is hoped to accelerate services, taking advantage of the new trains' superior performance, from May 2019.

porterbrook

MORE TRAINS, MORE ROUTES –
LONDON OVERGROUND'S CLASS 710

Transport for London's Overground operation has completely transformed services on long-neglected local railways in and around the capital. As the city's population grows and demand increases, its train fleet is expanding to create additional capacity and add more new routes.

lass 710 is a development of Bombardier's 'Aventra' family ordered for London Overground inner-suburban lines north and east of the capital. A £260 million contract to build 45 four-car trains was awarded in July 2015 (with an option for 24 more four-car sets, plus further option to extend some or all units to five cars) and the trains are due to enter service on the newly-electrified Gospel Oak-Barking route by November 2018.

As well as 'GOBLIN' services, the fleet has been acquired to help enhance frequencies and increase capacity on the North London and West London Lines, the Euston-Watford Junction 'DC Lines', and to replace ex-BR Class 315s and 317s on inner-suburban routes from Liverpool Street to Chingford, Cheshunt and Enfield Town. Additional trains are also required to extend 'GOBLIN' services to Barking Riverside by 2021 and, by releasing Class 378s, allow an increase in East London Line (ELL) services from 16 trains per hour (tph) to 20tph. London Overground services are operated by Arriva Rail London (ARL), a subsidiary of German national operator Deutsche Bahn, under a 7.5-year concession awarded by Transport for London (TfL) in November 2016.

TfL originally intended to procure a fleet of longer DMUs for Gospel Oak-Barking, as by 2012 the two-car Class 172/0 'Turbostar' units were unable to cope with demand, causing overcrowding throughout the day. TfL issued a tender for eight three-car or four-car trains, but this was shelved when authorisation

was given for the line to be electrified at 25kv AC overhead. Arriva Rail London's small fleet of DMUs will be cascaded to West Midlands Railway when the much-delayed electric service is finally introduced, increasing capacity on non-electrified routes around Birmingham from December.

Initially, the plan was for a total of 39 four-car EMUs, with 30 for the Liverpool Street routes, eight for Gospel Oak-Barking, and one for the Romford to Upminster shuttle.

The order was subsequently increased to 45 four-car EMUs, with the additional six units destined for the Watford 'DC lines'. This was to allow LOTrain to switch five-car Class 378s back to the North London and East London lines to deliver increased frequencies on these very busy routes.

In 2017, Transport for London put forward a proposal to procure a further nine Class 710s to be used as capacity enhancers. These took up 42 of the 249 additional vehicle options, and will be formed into three four-car sets for use on the extended 'GOBLIN' route to Barking Riverside, which is due to open in 2021, and six five-car trains for LO's North London and West London lines. A total of 54 trains are now being assembled at Bombardier's Derby plant.

SUB-FLEETS

The LO order is split into two sub-fleets: 31 AC-only Class 710/1s (Nos. 710101-131) for Liverpool Street services and Romford-Upminster and 23 dual-voltage Class 710/2s (of which Nos. 710256-272 are

four-car sets) for Gospel Oak-Barking (11 sets), the North London, West London and Euston lines. The six five-car trains will be deployed on the North London and West London lines, releasing Class 378s to increase frequencies on the East London Line to 20tph. As the new 'Aventras' do not have cab-end emergency doors, they cannot be used through the East London Line's tunnels under the River Thames.

Both sub-classes are closely related to the Class 345s being built for Crossrail (see page 24) and feature metro-style longitudinal seating. This will be something of a change for commuters to Enfield, Cheshunt and Chingford, but has been standard on other LO routes worked by '387s' for some years.

The AC-only trains will be maintained at Ilford depot in east London, while the dual-voltage sets will join their 'Capitalstar' cousins at Willesden TMD in north-west London. Initial testing was undertaken during 2017/18 in a controlled environment at Melton RIDC test track in the East Midlands. Testing in London started during summer 2018 after delivery of the first sets to Willesden depot.

TfL says that the trains will "transform the service experienced by customers on these routes", and will have similar features to the fleet that serves other parts of the London Overground network, including walk-through carriages, air-conditioning and improved accessibility – there will also be new features such as live TfL journey information.

Class 710s will also feature wider doors and full-width gangways to help passengers board and alight quicker, and move through the train

porterbrook

A brand-new Class 710/2 stands in the sun at Bombardier's Litchurch Lane works in Derby on June 28. The family resemblance to TfL Rail's Class 345s is clear, although there are many differences between the two designs. BEN JONES

Bombardier Class 710 'Aventra'

Built:	2017-18
Introduced:	November 2018
No. ordered:	54
No. of cars per train:	Four or five
Numbers:	710101-131, 710256-272, five-car sets TBC
Order value:	£260m
Power supply:	25kv AC overhead (710/1) or 25kv AC overhead and 750v DC third-rail (710/2)
Max speed:	90mph
Power rating:	TBC
Formation:	DMSO(A)+ MSO+ PMSO+ DMSO(B)
Capacity:	TBC
Features:	Air-conditioning, longitudinal metro-style seating, wide gangways within set, sliding plug doors
Routes:	Gospel Oak-Barking Riverside, Liverpool Street-Enfield/Chingford, Euston-Watford DC Lines, Romford-Upminster
Owner/finance:	Transport for London

Below: Bombardier assembly line staff install internal equipment in a Class 710 vehicle at Litchurch Lane on June 28. BEN JONES

A completed Class 710 Driving Car takes a ride on one of Litchurch Lane's traversers on June 28, moving from the assembly hall to another building for static tests before being united with the other three cars to form a complete set. BEN JONES

SIX-STAGE TEST PROCESS

Bombardier operates a six-stage test process for new trains assembled in Derby.

Stage 1 covers the sub-assemblies such as cabs, inner end cupboards, toilets and doors.

Stage 2 ensures that the saloon lighting, doors, antennae and CCTV equipment are all functioning correctly and puts every vehicle through a water spray test to check for any leaks.

That is followed by **stage 3** testing individual cars to check heating, ventilation and air-conditioning (HVAC) equipment, lights, passenger information systems (PIS), toilets, doors, brakes, levelling and air systems.

In **stage 4**, a split-unit test checks headlights, traction equipment, PIS, doors and brakes, before all the cars are brought together for **stage 5**. At this point, the complete train is united for the first time and door, braking, PIS and cab-to-cab communication systems are tested to ensure that the train is ready for dynamic testing in **stage 6**.

The final round of tests sees all new trains undergo low-speed dynamic testing on the short test track at Litchurch Lane, followed by higher-speed mileage accumulation runs at Network Rail's Melton Rail Industry Development Centre (RIDC) – the former BR Old Dalby test track. During this stage, propulsion equipment, brakes, signalling, train protection and advanced warning systems are checked, along with energy metering while the train performs endurance tests to 'shake out' any bugs before it is delivered to the operator to start work.

more easily. A novel feature is the provision of USB charging sockets in the walls of the wide gangway sections, allowing standing passengers to charge mobile devices.

However, despite the family resemblance to Class 345, there are some significant differences between the '345' and '710' vehicles. For example, the car lengths are slightly different to match existing LO trains and platform lengths and the traction equipment is arranged differently from Crossrail's trains. Class 710/1s will also be coupled to form eight-car trains at peak times in and out of Liverpool Street, whereas the '345s' are fixed formation nine-car sets.

Bombardier has also incorporated much of the experience gained from LO's Class 378s into the new trains. Since their introduction in 2009, the '378s' have been an essential part of Overground's success and the fleet now stands at 57 five-car sets. Some were built as three-cars, others as four-cars, but all have been extended to five vehicles since 2015. Experience with those trains is being built into the 'Aventra' fleet, both in terms of maintenance and the passenger environment.

The '710s' have similar interiors to the Class 378s, with a strong London Overground 'look', setting them apart from the Class 345s.

To look after the new fleet, Bombardier has invested in improved and additional maintenance facilities at Willesden and Ilford and is adding extra light servicing capacity at Chingford.

Unseen by passengers, but essential for the operator and Network Rail maintenance teams, the '710s' will feature overhead line and track monitoring equipment as standard. As with most modern trains, they will also have the ability to send diagnostic information back to their home depot, allowing technicians to monitor their condition, remotely fix faults and remove trains from service before problems occur – increasing reliability for passengers and reducing the potential for disruption. As technology is improving all the time, the '710s' are able to report back far more

data than the Class 378s, which themselves are able to provide maintenance teams with huge amounts of information. However, it's possible that the older LO trains will be updated to match the 'Aventras', with train control management systems (TCMS) being seen as a key area for upgrading.

The first eight Class 710/2s will be introduced on the 'GOBLIN' route by November, according to Arriva Rail London, with the Euston-Watford 'DC lines' next to benefit in early-2019 and finally the Liverpool Street suburban lines later next year.

By operating more frequent services with brighter, cleaner and safer trains and much-improved stations, London Overground has revolutionised train services around and across the capital over the last decade. The introduction of the Class 710s will continue that trend, by allowing a further increase in frequencies on the busiest lines. However,

it's the long-neglected 'GOBLIN' route that will feel the greatest benefit, swapping two-car diesel trains for faster, cleaner electric units twice the length of the trains they are replacing.

Inset: All 'Aventra' EMUs are mounted on Derby-designed FLEXX Eco lightweight bogies, saving around 30% in weight per bogie. BEN JONES

A painted, but not complete Class 710/1 driving car from set No. 710115 on one of the Litchurch Lane assembly lines on June 28. The vehicle is yet to receive its bogies or underframe equipment, but the interior is close to completion at this stage. BEN JONES

porterbrook

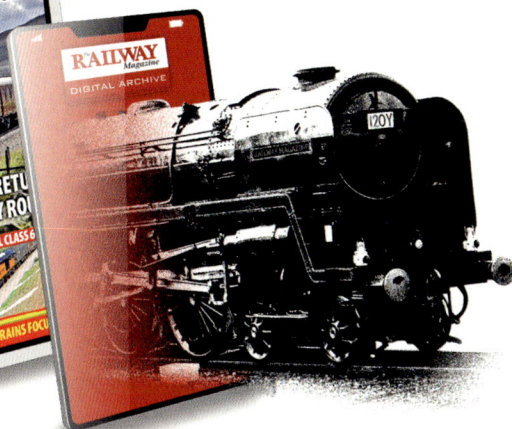

'AVENTRA': DERBY'S NEXT BIG SUCCESS STORY

Bombardier's latest EMU platform is well on the way to overtaking its hugely successful predecessor, the 'Electrostar' family, with thousands of vehicles ordered for delivery over the next few years.

GREATER ANGLIA CLASS 720

Operator:	Greater Anglia
Built:	2018-20
Introduced:	March/April 2019
No. ordered:	111 (89xfive-car, 22x10-car,
No. of cars per train:	Five/10 (665 vehicles)
Numbers:	720101-122 (10-car), 720501-589 (five-car)
Order value:	£900m
Routes:	Liverpool Street-Cambridge/Ipswich/Southend and branches
Power supply:	25kv AC overhead
Max speed:	100mph
Power rating:	TBC
Formation:	Class 720/1: DMSO+ PMSO(A)+ MSO(A)+ MSO(B)+ TSO + MSO(C)+ PMSO(B)+ MSO(D)+ MSO(E)+ DTSO, Class 720/5: DMSO+ PMSO+ MSO+ MSO+ DTSO
Capacity:	Class 720/1: 1146 seats, Class 720/5: 544 seats
Features:	Air-conditioning, wide gangways within set, sliding plug doors, wi-fi, at-seat plug and USB sockets, passenger information systems
Owner/finance:	Angel Trains/Bank of Australia

An artist's impression of Greater Anglia's Class 720/5, now being built in large numbers at Bombardier's Derby factory. GREATER ANGLIA

porterbrook

Greater Anglia Class 720/5 formation diagram. GREATER ANGLIA

Netherlands Railways subsidiary Abellio took the industry by surprise in August 2016 when, as part of its new Greater Anglia franchise, it opted to replace the entire existing fleet with new Bombardier and Stadler-built trains. The lion's share of that order went to Bombardier's Derby plant, with a massive £900 million order for 111 'Aventra' EMUs.

The Class 720s, formed into 89 five-car and 22 10-car trains will form a unified fleet and replace ex-BR Class 317s and 321s dating from the 1980s, early-2000s Siemens Class 360/1s and more recent Class 379 'Electrostars' on inner and outer-suburban routes radiating from London Liverpool Street to Essex, Suffolk and Cambridgeshire.

As part of the 'Aventra' family, the Class 720s will resemble Crossrail's Class 345s and Class 710s being constructed for Crossrail and London Overground respectively. However, the '720s' will have a higher maximum speed of 100mph, reflecting the longer-distance services they will work.

GA Aventras will work from Liverpool Street to Cambridge, Hertford East, Southend Victoria, Southminster, Braintree, Colchester, Clacton, Walton and Ipswich, supported by the Stadler FLIRTs working the Stansted Express and London-Norwich inter-city services. They will be maintained at Ilford depot and another facility yet to be decided. A new depot at Brantham, near Manningtree, was to have been completed in time to start receiving the new fleet for commissioning in late-2018, but this has been put on hold due to access problems. As this publication went to press, an alternative site in Harwich was being suggested.

The units will be fully air-conditioned, with seatback tables and at-seat power sockets, passenger-loading and capacity indicators providing real time data to the passenger information system and on-train wi-fi. Seating will be arranged in 3+2 and 2+2 suburban style,

with seats cantilevered from the wall to create more space for bags and make cleaning easier.

Five-car Class 720/5 sets will be 122m long and provide 544 seats, while their 10-car sisters will have a whopping 1146 seats, highlighting their intended role as peak-time 'crowdbusters'.

Variations of the 'Aventra' platform are being built for several different customers but, according to Bombardier, the Class 720 is one of the most densely populated vehicles it has yet designed.

The 665 cars are designed to carry as many people as possible, a key factor of Abellio's bid to retain the East Anglia franchise (from 2016 to 2025) on the basis of strong passenger growth over the coming years. The Class 720s will individually carry between 22% and 45% more people than the current fleet. The walk-through 'Aventra' cars will have 3+2 and 2+2 seating configurations, as well as fold-down chairs and areas for wheelchair users. Perhaps controversially, the Class 720s will not include First Class accommodation – another compromise to ensure increased seating capacity.

The '720s' will allow GA to increase capacity while reducing the number of cars per train at the same time – reducing weight and maintenance costs. The cars are longer than the current fleet at 24m rather than 20m – making the 10-car variant comparable in size to a 12-car Class 321 formation.

An interior mock-up was unveiled by Greater Anglia in September 2017, following a consultation with passenger groups and members of the public. Changes to the original specification included replacing the proposed Fainsa seating with softer seating and the addition of seatback tables – the omission of which from Thameslink Class 700s has been the cause of much criticism.

Passenger information systems will display where space is available on a train, whether toilets are available, journey progression and updates for onward journeys by main line and London Underground services.

Assembly of the first vehicles began at Litchurch Lane in February 2018 and the first completed set was expected to be unveiled in August. Deliveries will commence in January 2019 and the first five-car trains are due to enter service two months later. Five-car Class 720/5s will be first

Far left: Class 720 interior with 3+2 seating and wide gangways for outer-suburban commuter traffic on the Great Eastern and West Anglia routes. GREATER ANGLIA

Left: Class 720 accessible toilet and multi-purpose space with flip-up seats. When not being used by passengers in wheelchairs, this area can be used for bikes or pushchairs. GREATER ANGLIA

Abellio has ordered three variants of the 'Aventra' family for its West Midlands Railway franchise. Two will supplement existing 110mph Siemens fleets on West Coast Main Line services, while the other will replace ex-BR Class 323s on Birmingham's Cross-City route.
BOMBARDIER

Above: A driving car from Greater Anglia five-car 'Aventra' No. 720503 nears completion at Litchurch Lane works in Derby on June 28. GA has 89 five-car and 22 10-car Class 720s on order for delivery in 2019-21.
BEN JONES

WEST MIDLANDS CLASS 730/731/732

Operator:	London North Western/ West Midlands Railway
Built:	2020-22
Introduced:	2020
No. ordered:	81 (45xfive-car, 36xthree-car)
No. of cars per train:	Five/three
Numbers:	TBC
Order Value:	£542m
Routes:	Euston-Birmingham/ Liverpool, Lichfield-Redditch/Bromsgrove, Coventry-Birmingham-Walsall/Wolverhampton
Power supply:	25kv AC overhead
Max Speed:	100/90mph
Power rating:	TBC
Formation:	TBC
Capacity:	TBC
Features:	Air-conditioning, wide gangways within set, sliding plug doors, wi-fi, at-seat plug and USB sockets, passenger information systems
Owner/finance:	Infracapital/Deutsche Asset Management

production line, with 10-car sets following that, although at least one pre-series train is expected to be built in advance of the series batch.

In order to deliver the huge number of 'Aventra' vehicles due to enter service over the next three years, Bombardier will double the rate of production in Derby in early-2019, from the current 12 cars per week to an unprecedented 24.

They will also feature at least one standard and one accessible toilet per set and four cycle spaces. Bombardier's hugely successful 'Flexx Eco' lightweight bogies provide a 30% reduction in bogie mass, which across a 10-car train saves a considerable amount of weight and energy.

By 2020, commuters on the Great Eastern Main Line and West Anglia lines will be travelling on a completely new fleet of trains and should notice a significant advance in facilities over the ex-BR trains dating from the 1980s. Learning lessons from current complaints about comfort, the Class 720 seats also promise to be more comfortable. Their high-density arrangement promises more passengers the opportunity of getting a seat at peak times, but will they prove to be more popular than other new trains currently being introduced?

LTS EXPANSION

In December 2017, Trenitalia's c2c franchise ordered six 10-car Bombardier 'Aventra' sets to increase capacity on its busy London, Tilbury & Southend (LTS) commuter routes. The new trains are designated Class 711. Due to enter service in summer 2021, the 240m-long trains will displace six four-car Class 387s leased from Porterbrook since 2017. These trains, ordered speculatively by the leasing company, were introduced to bring forward improvements instigated by the new franchise owner after it acquired c2c from National Express.

c2c's original intention was to procure a further 68 EMU vehicles to expand its fleet, formed into 17 four-car sets as part of its Essex Thameside franchise agreement.

However, in 2017, c2c announced it had agreed a £105m deal with Bombardier and Porterbrook to obtain 60 'Aventra' vehicles formed into six 10-car trains. The longer vehicles of the new design will allow increased capacity (940 seats) over a 12-car formation but with fewer vehicles – reducing weight and maintenance requirements.

Bombardier will also provide eight years

porterbrook

of maintenance and support services from their introduction until November 2029.

"The deal demonstrates our focus on long-term investments in the UK market and our desire to constantly improve the standing of our trains and to deliver visible and valuable improvements on our services," said Ernesto Sicilia, managing director of c2c parent company Trenitalia UK when the contract was announced in December 2017.

"Since our entrance into the UK market, the original new trains investment plan, which included a phased delivery from 2019 to 2024, has been accelerated. We are extremely proud that the new fleet will start to be delivered from summer 2021, three years earlier than originally planned."

In common with their sisters ordered by Greater Anglia and West Midlands Railway, the 100mph 25kv AC train units will feature high density seating, air-conditioning, wi-fi, real time passenger and loading information, at-seat plug

sockets and wide gangways between cars, allowing passengers to move more freely through the trains.

They will work alongside the existing Class 357 fleet, also built at Derby as an early member of the 'Electrostar' family, providing much-needed extra seating capacity for LTS commuters. It remains to be seen what will happen to the Class 387s leased as an interim measure, although with hundreds of similar units working for various operators, including GWR, Southern and Great Northern, they should have no problem finding a new home.

WEST MIDLANDS RAILWAY

Following its retention of Greater Anglia, Abellio scored another success in late-2017 by winning the West Midlands franchise previously held by Govia. Again, a central part of its winning offer – in a joint venture between JR East and Mitsui of Japan – was a large fleet of new trains, although not a complete fleet replacement in this case.

Once again, Bombardier's 'Aventra' took the major share of the new order with a total of 333 25kv AC overhead EMU vehicles ordered.

Reflecting the dual nature of the London Northwestern/West Midlands Railway operation, these will be formed into three separate types. For Birmingham-area suburban routes there will be 36 Class 730 three-car high capacity 'Metro' units to replace the current Class 323s from 2020. Also on order are 29 five-car 110mph units for Euston outer-suburban services and 16 more five-car 110mph sets for Euston-Northampton-Birmingham semi-fast services (provisionally Class 731/732). The latter will supplement the current Siemens Class 350/1 EMUs based at Northampton, but the high-density Class 350/2s – Britain's most reliable EMUs – will be returned to the leasing company when all the new trains are in service from 2021.

"Being selected for this important order is another huge endorsement of our workforce and the quality of the products we design, engineer and manufacture here in the UK," said Richard Hunter, UK managing director, Bombardier Transportation.

"Our modern Aventra trains will be built in the Midlands for the Midlands and provide passengers with greater connectivity, reliability and shorter journey times."

More information is expected to be released about these new trains in 2019.

Below: An artist's impression of the 'Aventra' variant being built for c2c. These 10-car trains will add much-needed extra capacity on commuter routes from Essex into London Fenchurch Street.
BOMBARDIER

Inset: A computer-generated image of the proposed interior layout of the c2c 'Aventra' showing the 3+2 commuter seating layout that will give each train 940 seats.
BOMBARDIER

C2C CLASS 711

Operator:	c2c
Built:	2020-21
Introduced:	2021
No. ordered:	60 vehicles
No. of cars per train:	10
Numbers:	TBC
Order value:	£105m
Routes:	Fenchurch Street-Southend-Shoeburyness
Power supply:	25kv AC overhead
Max speed:	100mph
Power rating:	See Class 720/5
Formation:	See Class 720/5
Capacity:	940 seats
Features:	Air-conditioning, wide gangways within set, sliding plug doors, wi-fi, at-seat plug and USB sockets, passenger information systems
Owner/finance:	Porterbrook

Turn to page 38 to see more variants of the Bombardier 'Aventra' family.

porterbrook

SOUTH WESTERN
PREPARES FOR WATERLOO 'METRO' OPERATION

An artist's impression of a South Western Railway (SWR) Class 701, 90 of which will be delivered by Bombardier for Waterloo suburban routes in 2019-20. Assembly work is already underway on the first trains in Derby.
BOMBARDIER TRANSPORTATION

Serving Britain's busiest commuter routes, First/MTR's South Western Railway franchise chose the Bombardier 'Aventra' to help it deliver more peak-time seats and more trains as the Waterloo suburban lines move towards metro-style frequencies.

S hortly after securing the lucrative South Western franchise from Stagecoach in March 2017, FirstGroup and MTR of Hong Kong placed a massive order for new electric trains with Bombardier in Derby. It was another huge success for the 'Aventra' platform, adding another 750 vehicles to the Litchurch Lane order book and securing thousands of jobs in Derby and the wider supply chain across the UK and Europe.

Continuing the trend for winning bids containing major fleet replacement programmes, First/MTR chose to procure a new standard fleet for commuter routes radiating out from Waterloo to Reading and Windsor and serving the south-western suburbs of the capital.

This decision surprised many, given that South West Trains already had a reasonably modern, if diverse, fleet of EMUs, ranging from ex-BR Class 455s and 456s dating from the 1980s (many of which have been modernised with new traction packages in the last few years), to Alstom Class 458s and early-2000s Siemens Class 450 'Desiro' units. Even more surprising was First/MTR's rejection of 150 new Siemens Class 707 vehicles (30 five-car trains), ordered by Stagecoach for SWT, but not

SW
R

porterbrook

BOMBARDIER CLASS 701

Operator:	First/MTR South Western Railway
Built:	2019-20
Introduced:	2019
No. ordered:	90 (30xfive-car, 60x10-car)
No. of cars per train:	Five/10 (750 vehicles)
Numbers:	701001-060 (10-car), 701501-530 (five-car)
Order value:	£895m
Routes:	Waterloo-Reading/ Windsor, SW London suburban lines
Power supply:	750v DC third-rail (3x dual-voltage test sets)
Max speed:	100mph
Power rating:	TBC
Formation:	DM+(P)M+TLW+M+EM+ EM+M+TLW+(P)M+DM (701/0)
Capacity:	Class 701/0: 556 seats, 740 standing (total 1296), Class 701/5: 269 seats, 330 standing
Features:	Air-conditioning, wide gangways within set, wi-fi, at-seat plug sockets, sliding plug doors, colour passenger information systems, wide gangways, full width cab, regenerative braking, one bio-reactor universal access toilet per set
Owner/finance:	Rock Rail

Interior view showing the large circulating area around the doors to allow faster access and egress from the new trains and extra space for standing passengers at busy times. BOMBARDIER TRANSPORTATION

even in service when the franchise changed hands (see page 41).

With Waterloo suburban routes a priority for Network Rail's 'Digital Railway' programme, which will eventually see trains controlled by European Train Control System (ETCS) in-cab signalling and Automatic Train Operation (ATO) to increase capacity on the busiest lines, the decision to focus on a common fleet with identical performance characteristics hints at the metro-style frequencies

Below: An artist's impression of how a Class 701 car will look in South Western Railway livery. BOMBARDIER TRANSPORTATION

that will be delivered in and out of Waterloo in the 2020s. According to First/MTR, the new trains will boost peak capacity at Waterloo by 46%.

COMMON FLEET

After placing the order in June 2017, FirstGroup Rail managing director Steve Montgomery said: "We have exciting plans for the South Western rail franchise and these new trains are an important step on the way. We know from listening to passengers and stakeholders that alongside improved performance, what they want to see is additional seats and we will deliver this via these state-of-the-art trains."

Materials for the Class 701s started to arrive at Bombardier's Derby plant in July 2018, with assembly of the first sets taking place over the second half of the year. South Western Railway (SWR) will start taking delivery of its first 'Aventras' in 2019 and they are due to enter service in 2019-20 on the Reading, Windsor and south-west London suburban lines. All are expected to be in service by December 2020.

To meet this challenging schedule, Bombardier will have to double production from the current 12 'Aventra' vehicles per week to 24 from early-2019.

The 750 vehicles will be marshalled into 90 Class 701 trains, 60 fixed 10-car sets

(Nos. 701001-060) and 30 five-car sets (Nos. 701501-530), which will also be able to operate in multiple to form 10-car trains.

The new fleet will be maintained at SWR's Wimbledon depot with technical assistance and spares support from Bombardier for the duration of the seven-year franchise. There is an option to extend the support agreement if the franchise is extended.

Three sets will be delivered as dual-voltage trains with 25kv AC overhead equipment, as well as 750v DC third-rail shoegear. This will not be required in normal service, but will be used to demonstrate the dual-voltage capability of the '701s'.

Like their sisters being built for London Overground, Greater Anglia, c2c and West Midlands, the trains will feature aluminium bodies and inside-framed Bombardier 'FLEXX ECO' bogies to reduce weight, wide gangways between cars, wide doors to facilitate rapid boarding and alighting, 2+2 seating, free wi-fi, at-seat USB charging points, real-time passenger information screens, air-conditioning and one wheelchair-accessible toilet per five-car section. The trains will also have regenerative braking, reducing energy costs by returning electricity to the grid during braking.

Funding for the SWR 'Aventras' is coming

porterbrook

from Rock Rail and partners SL Capital (part of Standard Life Investments) and GLIL Infrastructure LLP, working with a consortium of UK, European and North American institutional investors.

MOVING OUT

The introduction of the Class 701s will completely change the face of Waterloo suburban services over the next two years. As well as the controversial rejection of the Class 707s (see page 41), SWR's Class 455 four-car and Class 456 two-car suburban units will be returned to their owner – Porterbrook Leasing. These ex-British Rail sets dating from the 1980s are well into their third decade, but all have been extensively refurbished and many '455s' now have modern AC traction and control equipment fitted at great expense over the last few years. It's likely that at least some of these will move on to pastures new if good homes can be found or Porterbrook can adapt them for new uses.

Also subject to costly modifications in recent years is the GEC-Alsthom-built Class 458 fleet, also owned by Porterbrook. A combination of Class 458 and 460 vehicles built for SWT and Gatwick Express in 1998-2000, and rebuilt by Wabtec Doncaster and

Right: The Class 701s will replace all existing SWR inner-suburban EMUs, including the 30 Siemens-built '707s', built in 2016/17. KEITH FENDER

Brush in Loughborough in 2013-16, they are now formed into five-car Standard Class-only sets for Waterloo commuter lines. As a non-standard fleet they face an uncertain future.

However, the trains arriving in their place promise better facilities for Waterloo commuters, a more modern environment, more frequent services and more seats, not to mention allowing SWR to deliver

a more consistent product on its key suburban routes. Once the 'Digital Railway' enhancements promised by Network Rail are in place in the 2020s, we could see automatically controlled Class 701s providing a high-frequency 'metro' service across south-west London and into Surrey and Berkshire, potentially delivering faster, more frequent journeys for long-suffering commuters.

BOMBARDIER

Above: Class 701 interior view showing the high-density seating layout. BOMBARDIER TRANSPORTATION

Below: A five-car Class 701 in SWR livery. BOMBARDIER TRANSPORTATION

porterbrook

LOOKING FOR A NEW HOME - ONE CAREFUL OWNER!

When the South Western franchise came up for renewal, the expectation was that the 30 Siemens-built 'Desiro City' Class 707s procured by Stagecoach would be retained by South Western, alongside its existing fleets of Class 450s. However, the '707s' are said to be more expensive to lease than the new 'Aventras', and FirstGroup and MTR's decision to change the fleet policy has meant that 150 Class 707 vehicles, which entered service between late-2017 and spring 2018, have no obvious operator after 2019, when the initial lease ends.

This cut-off date was designed to coincide with the end of an extended SWT franchise, had negotiations with the Department for Transport (DfT) for a two-year direct award been successful. However, those talks failed with the result that a £200 million fleet of nearly-new EMUs will be redundant after less than two years in service with SWR.

As with many modern trains, the modular Class 707s can be converted to 25kv overhead operation if required and test running included trials with Nos. 707001/002 working in dual voltage mode over the Thameslink network. The trains are a derivative of Thameslink's Class 700s, so it is feasible that they could find a home away from the third-rail network. Certainly, Angel Trains, their owner, will be keen to find a new home for this expensive asset.

The DfT distanced itself from SWR's change of fleet policy, saying: "First MTR has committed to deliver 750 new carriages by the end of 2020, which will offer more space and improve journeys. It is for First MTR South Western to decide how it uses its trains."

At the time of the franchise change, the General Secretary of the RMT union, Mick Cash, said that First MTR's decision was a "cast-iron example of the crazy world of rail privatisation," and called on the Government to undertake an urgent investigation into the commissioning process for the rolling stock.

He added: "No one knows what is going to happen to the dumped rolling stock and what the cost of this fiasco is going to be. This is a scandal of huge proportions."

However, in the meantime, the Siemens-built Class 707s are providing much-needed additional capacity on SWR's routes from Waterloo to Windsor, Weybridge and Hounslow. An extra 5000 seats per day are now being provided on Waterloo suburban routes with 10-car trains provided instead of the previous eight-car sets. The 30 five-car '707s' have released other trains for Reading line services, in turn freeing Class 450s and 458s to transfer to suburban and main line routes to help boost capacity elsewhere.

The additional services have been made possible by Network Rail's work to extend platforms and increase capacity at Waterloo in August 2017 as part of an £800m scheme to increase capacity at London's busiest station.

Top: Gloomy forecast: Despite only entering service in early-2018, the 30 five-car Class 707 EMUs now in use with South Western Railway will be redundant by the end of 2020. They are currently employed in five and 10-car formations, helping to add 5000 extra seats on Waterloo suburban routes. On June 1, No. 707020 calls at Vauxhall under stormy skies with a service bound for Waterloo. BEN JONES

Bottom: Closely related to the Thameslink Class 700s, the Siemens-built Class 707s are also capable of working from 25kv AC overhead with the addition of a pantograph and modifications to traction equipment. Could they end up working alongside their cousins on cross-London services? No. 707005 arrives at Clapham Junction with a Windsor Line service on June 1. BEN JONES

porterbrook

INTER-CITY:
A NEW GENERA

Forty years on from the InterCity 125 revolution, a new generation of high-tech trains is entering service on key long-distance routes, delivering improvements for passengers from Cornwall to the Highlands of Scotland.

porterbrook

TION STEPS UP

One of GWR's new Class 800 bi-mode Intercity Express Trains, No. 800004 *Isambard Kingdom Brunel*, is put through its paces on the recently electrified Great Western Main Line. Since October 2017, these trains have been in passenger service between London, Bristol and South Wales. GWR

porterbrook

INTERCITY EXPRESS TRAIN

Hitachi's IET test programme has taken pre-series trains to every part of the GWR and East Coast networks, including destinations served by limited services, such as Glasgow, and diversionary routes. GWR green five-car bi-mode No. 800004 *Isambard Kingdom Brunel* makes an unusual sight at Glasgow Central during a test run in early-2018. GWR

Inset: The Standard Class interior of the GWR Class 800-802, showing the airy, if spartan, saloon and the 'firm' seats that have been the subject of some criticism from passengers. BEN JONES

A new fleet of Japanese-designed trains is steadily replacing the iconic InterCity 125s on the Great Western and East Coast main lines, bringing bi-mode technology to inter-city routes from London to South Wales, the west of England, Yorkshire, the north-east and Scotland.

porterbrook

HITACHI CLASS 800/801 IET

Operator:	GWR/LNER
Built:	2013-19
Introduced:	October 2017 (GWR), December 2018 (LNER)
No. ordered:	122 (866 vehicles)
No. of cars per train:	Five/nine
Numbers:	See separate panel
Order value:	£4.5bn
Routes:	Paddington-Bristol/ South Wales/Cotswold Line (GWR), King's Cross-Yorkshire/ Newcastle/Scotland (LNER)
Power supply:	25kv AC overhead/ diesel (Class 800), 25kv AC electric (Class 801)
Max speed:	125mph (140mph design speed)
Formation:	See separate panel
Capacity:	308 seats (five-car), 698 seats (nine-car)
Features:	Air-conditioning, fast-acting sliding doors, gangways within set, wi-fi, at-seat charging points, bi-mode electric/diesel operation,
Owner/finance:	Agility Trains

Forty years after their introduction, the legendary InterCity 125s are finally starting to be replaced. Since 1976, HSTs have been the backbone of British long-distance passenger operation. Their dominance is starting to come to an end though, thanks to a new generation of high-speed trains now being built by Hitachi Rail Europe.

In summer 2012, the Department for Transport (DfT) finally agreed a £4.5 billion deal for HST replacement trains – known as the Intercity Express Programme, or IEP. A consortium of Japanese conglomerate Hitachi and civil engineering giant John Laing won the right to design, finance, build and maintain two fleets of trains, totalling 122 sets (866 vehicles), to replace existing stock on the Great Western (57 sets) and East Coast Main Lines (65 sets).

The Great Western Railway (GWR) fleet is a mix of bi-mode five-car and nine-car trains with 25kv AC overhead electric equipment and underfloor MTU diesel engines, while Virgin Trains East Coast will have both five/nine-car bi-modes and nine-car 25kv AC electric sets. However, even the latter will feature a single diesel engine, allowing them to be shunted 'off the wires' or run at low speed to the nearest station if there's a problem with the electric supply.

GWR was originally scheduled to have both bi-mode and electric sets, but in mid-2016 the order was changed in response to delays on Network Rail's Great Western Main Line upgrade. This means that more diesel working is now necessary than was previously anticipated, including between Cardiff and Swansea and at various points between Swindon and Bristol.

On October 16, 2017, the first GWR Class 800/0 five-car sets entered passenger service on the Paddington-Bristol/South Wales routes. While the launch was not entirely trouble-free, the trains are steadily usurping GWR's HSTs. The first of 21 nine-car Class 800/3s entered passenger service in June 2018, joining the 36 '800/0s' that have gradually gained more diagrams over the first half of the year.

In December 2018, the first East Coast Main Line (ECML) Intercity Express Trains (IETs) are expected to be introduced on the King's Cross-Leeds/Hull routes, replacing London North Eastern Railway (LNER) HSTs and Class 91+Mk4 IC225 sets.

GLOBAL PROJECT

Twelve pre-series were built at Hitachi's factory in Kasado, Japan, but the rest of the IEP order is being assembled at the company's £82 million facility in Newton Aycliffe, Co. Durham. Bodyshells are shipped in large quantities from Kasado to be fitted out in County Durham with components from Japan, the UK and across Europe.

porterbrook

Designated 'Super Express Train' (SET) by Hitachi, they are based on the company's 'A-Train' concept and related to Southeastern's Class 395 'Javelin' EMUs. They also share many components with Hitachi 'Bullet Trains' for Japanese railways.

Close to the birthplace of modern railways in the north-east of England, Hitachi has built a vast assembly plant employing more than 1200 people. Of those, around 850 are directly involved in transforming the painted bodyshells that arrive from Japan into fully-functioning IETs. Although more than 50% of the critical work is completed in Japan, there is still much to do when the bodyshells arrive at Newton Aycliffe.

Each Class 800/801 vehicle takes 29 days to finish, moving through a cleverly designed and tightly organised production line. Cars spend roughly one day at various 'stations', each of which is dedicated to a specific task, from electrics to installation of heating, ventilation and air-conditioning (HVAC) modules, gangways and power units.

Towards the end of the process, the vehicle is lowered onto its bogies and moved into its final position for fitting the interior. On the 30th and final day of the build, the completed vehicle moves to the testing bay for final checking. Once this thorough inspection is complete, the vehicle can be brought together with its companions to form a full train, which then undertakes low-speed runs on the factory's short test track.

Main line approval runs then follow, with sets running over the ECML to Hitachi's new depot in Doncaster initially, and then to the customer for acceptance trials.

At 26m-long, Class 800-802 cars are the first British passenger vehicles with bodyshells longer than the previous 23m (75ft) 'C3' restriction. To fit within the existing 'envelope' the cars are noticeably tapered at each end.

TESTING TIMES

Since the first sets arrived in the UK in March 2015, pre-series IEP trains have been undergoing testing to gain approval for use on the Network Rail system. Much of this work took place at Network Rail's Rail Innovation and Development Centre (RIDC) near Melton Mowbray in 2014/15. This former BR Railway Technical Centre (RTC) test track offers 13 miles of dedicated line fit for 125mph testing between Old Dalby and Edwalton, on the outskirts of Nottingham.

Away from the congested national network, engineers checked that the Class 800s and 801s complied with all necessary specifications and rules for performance, noise, braking, adhesion, electromagnetic compatibility with signalling and other lineside equipment and dozens of other factors.

However, from late-2015, sorties out onto the national network became increasingly regular and new IETs and Class 802s are now a common sight making delivery and test runs on the ECML and GW main line.

October 2016 saw the type make its debut in Devon, with nine-car 800101 making test runs to Plymouth. Hitachi Rail Europe has leased the former Eurostar depot at North Pole in west London as its base in southern England. Over the last two years, test runs (often overnight) have been made to all the routes expected to see IETs and AT300s, from Penzance, West Wales and Hereford to Glasgow, Aberdeen and Inverness and many diversionary routes where the trains also need to be cleared for operation.

In May 2018, Network Rail and Virgin Trains East Coast announced that they had cleared all East Coast Main Line and diversionary routes for Class 800/801 operation.

So far, passenger reaction to the new trains is reported to be largely positive, although many observers have commented on the surprisingly firm seats, especially in Standard Class. While GWR says the feedback it is receiving from customers is positive about the seats, there continues to be adverse comment from many passengers on social media.

LNER (formerly Virgin Trains East Coast) passengers will get their first taste of the new generation in December when the first Class 800/2 five-car sets are introduced on the King's Cross-Leeds/Hull routes. These will be followed by the 13 nine-car Class 800/1s and the electric Class 801/1s (five-car) and 801/2s (nine-car).

While the 42 electric-only trains will replace IC225s and HSTs on King's Cross-Leeds/Newcastle/Edinburgh services, LNER's bi-mode sets will be deployed on Hull, Lincoln, Sunderland, Aberdeen and Inverness services, all of which have non-electrified sections and are currently worked by HSTs.

Although it was stripped of the franchise in May 2018, Virgin Trains East Coast also promised to extend Class 800 operation to provide direct trains between King's Cross, Middlesbrough and Huddersfield from December 2019. It remains to be seen whether these, and other timetable enhancements promised by VTEC, can now be delivered, especially as various ECML capacity enhancements needed

INTERCITY EXPRESS TRAIN (IET) FLEET

Great Western Railway

Class 800/0:	Five-car bi-mode IEP (25kv AC/diesel)
	800001-036
	DTRBFO+MSO+MSO+MSO+DTSO
Built:	2013-18. In service.
Class 800/3:	Nine-car bi-mode IEP (25kv AC/diesel)
	801301-321
	DTRBFO+MFO+MCO+MSO+MSO+MSO+MSO+MSO+DTSO
Built:	2013-18. Entering service.

London North Eastern Railway

Class 800/1:	Nine-car bi-mode IEP (25kv AC/diesel)
	800101-113
	DTRBFO+MFO+MCO+MSO+MSO+MSO+MSO+MSO+DTSO
Built:	2013-18. Introduction in 2018/19.
Class 800/2:	Five-car bi-mode IEP (25kv AC/diesel)
	800201-210
	DTRBFO+MSO+MSO+MSO+DTSO
Built:	2016-18. Introduction in 2018
Class 801/1:	Five-car electric IEP (25kv AC)
	801101-112
	DTRBFO+MSO+MSO+MSO+DTSO
Built:	2016-18. Introduction in 2019
Class 801/2:	Nine-car electric IEP (25kv AC)
	800201-230
	DTRBFO+MFO+MCO+MSO+MSO+MSO+MSO+MSO+DTSO
Built:	2017-19. Introduction in 2019

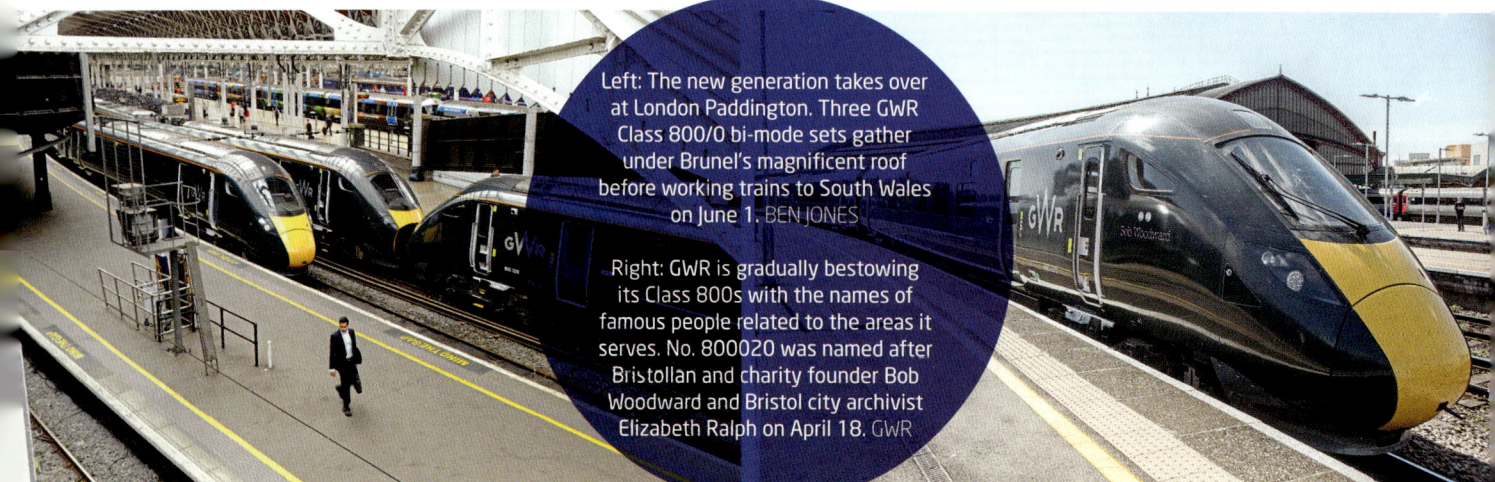

Left: The new generation takes over at London Paddington. Three GWR Class 800/0 bi-mode sets gather under Brunel's magnificent roof before working trains to South Wales on June 1. BEN JONES

Right: GWR is gradually bestowing its Class 800s with the names of famous people related to the areas it serves. No. 800020 was named after Bristollan and charity founder Bob Woodward and Bristol city archivist Elizabeth Ralph on April 18. GWR

A pre-series nine-car IET in Virgin Trains colours crosses the Royal Border Bridge at Berwick-upon-Tweed during East Coast Main Line testing. In June 2018, Network Rail announced that it had completed clearance work across more than 1700 miles of route that will be used by East Coast IETs. NETWORK RAIL

Below left: The new face of GWR, as a Class 387 'Electrostar' and a Class 800 approach London Paddington from the west at Royal Oak on June 1. By the end of 2019, almost all trains serving Paddington will be electric, significantly reducing diesel emissions in this area of London. BEN JONES

Below right: Intercity Express Train vehicles being fitted out at Hitachi Rail Europe's Newton Aycliffe factory in County Durham in October 2017. BEN JONES

for the 2019 timetable are now in doubt.

However, NR has delivered a large number of smaller enhancements along the routes to be served by IETs, including platform extensions at locations including Stevenage, Northallerton, Durham and Edinburgh Waverley, a major power supply upgrade between Wood Green and Doncaster on the East Coast Main Line, with a second phase between Doncaster and Edinburgh in preparation.

As IETs are longer and have a different cross section to the trains currently in use, gauge clearance was needed across more than 1700 miles of route, including 3000 sets of switches and crossings and 800 bridges and structures. These encompass London King's Cross to Inverness, Aberdeen, Leeds, Hull, Harrogate, Skipton and Glasgow, as well as diversionary routes such as London to Peterborough via Ely and Newcastle to Glasgow via Carlisle.

In addition, the project had to make more than 40 separate modifications on the route. These ranged enormously in scale from simple relocation of pieces of lineside equipment such as ground signals and speed signs that took a few hours, to much larger modifications taking several months, such as the demolition and reconstruction of platforms and bridges.

The second key milestone is the removal of a number of electrical boosters that are incompatible with the new trains.

Critical to the safe running and overhead line compatibility of the new trains, the project saw 35 overlap booster transformers, which channel traction return current into the return conductor, removed from 12 locations, ranging from Finsbury Park in London to Berwick-Upon-Tweed in Northumberland. An added benefit of the project is the recycling of the booster transformers north of Newcastle.

Elsewhere, in addition to the troubled and much-delayed electrification and resignalling of the GWML, which was curtailed by the Government after going far over its original budget, NR is undertaking many smaller projects to accommodate the new fleet, including gauge clearance schemes, station improvements and, around Bristol, a major resignalling and capacity enhancement scheme.

BUILD AND MAINTAIN

Pre-series trains were also used to commission several new depots and train maintenance staff who will be caring for them as part of the 27½-year contract. Major new 'mothership' depots are now fully operational at Stoke Gifford near Bristol for the GWR fleet and Doncaster for VTEC, TransPennine Express (TPE) and Hull Trains.

Existing depots at Craigentinny (Edinburgh), Swansea Maliphant and Bounds Green and North Pole in London have been modernised to accommodate the new trains, along with numerous depots and stabling points at other strategic locations from Penzance to Inverness.

By 2020, long-distance travel on the Great Western and East Coast routes will have been transformed by these new trains. Will they prove to be as successful and popular as the InterCity 125s? Will they deliver the 'Japanese' levels of reliability their builder has promised?

porterbrook

AT300: REACHING THE PARTS OTHER BI-MODES CAN'T

Developed from the Intercity Express Train, Hitachi's AT300 bi-mode is designed for sustained running in diesel mode and is being built to provide new trains for the west of England, trans-Pennine routes and Hull Trains.

I n 2015 GWR placed an additional £361 million order for 29 uprated bi-mode Hitachi AT300 units (173 vehicles) to work over the Devon banks to Plymouth and Penzance. A further seven nine-car Class 802 sets were added to the order in August 2016, taking GWR's total bi-mode fleet to 91 trains.

The AT300s fall outside the original Government-procured IEP fleet but will be closely related, featuring uprated engines and larger fuel tanks to cope with sustained diesel operation and to negotiate steeply graded lines in Devon and Cornwall. As Newton Aycliffe is working at full capacity on IEP and other new train orders, GWR's AT300s are being built in Italy at the Hitachi Rail Europe – formerly AnsaldoBreda – plant in Pistoia.

The trains are expected to reduce journey times from Paddington to Exeter by up to five minutes, to Plymouth by up to six minutes, and to Penzance by up to 14 minutes.

ITALIAN JOB

February 8 saw the first two completed Class 802 bi-mode trains unveiled to VIPs and the media at Hitachi Rail Europe's plant in Tuscany.

Five-car AT300s Nos. 802003 and 802004 (T4/T5) were the first of 33 trains built in Pistoia to replace InterCity 125s on Great Western Railway's (GWR) Paddington-West of England route. A total of 22 five-car '802/0s' and 14 nine-car '802/1s' have been ordered, financed by Eversholt Rail, with modifications to cater for the longer journeys to Devon and Cornwall and greater use on diesel power over hillier routes. Three Japanese-built pre-series trains (T1-T3) have been on test in the UK since 2017.

Nos. 802003/004 left Pistoia in late-February for the six-day journey to the UK. Hitachi is delivering one train roughly every 12-14 days by rail during 2018, with the last due in January 2019. RailAdventure, the German operator specialising in the delivery of new trains, has the contract to haul the new trains through Austria, Germany and France to the

porterbrook

Hitachi AT300 Fleet

Great Western Railway

Class 802/0:	Five-car bi-mode AT300 (25kv AC/diesel) 802001-022
Built:	2017-19
Class 802/1:	Nine-car bi-mode AT300 (25kv AC/diesel) 802101-114
Built:	2017-19

TransPennine Express

Class 802/2:	Five-car bi-mode AT300 (25kv AC/diesel) 19 sets – number series 802201-219.
Built:	2018-19. Introduction in December 2019

Hull Trains

Class 802/3:	Five-car bi-mode AT300 (25kv AC/diesel) Five sets – number series 802301-305.
Built:	2018-19

The first two completed GWR Class 802 five-car bi-mode sets roll out of the test hall at Hitachi Rail Europe's Pistoia factory in Italy in February. These trains are now being delivered to the UK and were due to make their debut in passenger service in July. BEN JONES

Channel Tunnel. Five-car sets are being delivered in pairs, with the nine-car '802/1s' travelling solo.

The tight delivery schedule calls for all 36 trains to be in traffic by March 2019, but the first sets were expected to make their passenger debut on GWR's 07.30 Paddington-Penzance on July 16. An option for a further seven nine-car Class 802/2s was taken up in August 2016 after it became clear that more bi-mode trains would be needed to support the Class 800 IET fleet on fast trains to Oxford and Bedwyn following the curtailment of Network Rail's GW electrification programme.

FLATPACK

By mid-February, bodyshells for trains up to T25 were under assembly at Pistoia. All 22 five-car trains are under construction and work is under way on the nine-car sets. In contrast to HRE's Newton Aycliffe plant in the UK, which receives part-finished bodyshells from Japan, the Italian factory assembles the aluminium bodies from flatpack kits produced by Hitachi's Kasado plant. Each set takes around 40 days to build.

After low-speed and static tests in Italy, the first three '802s' had to complete 5000 miles of fault-free running in the UK, reduced to 1000 miles for later sets.

The '802' specification includes MTU diesel power packs rated at their full 940hp – as opposed to the 750hp of the original IET specification –

and 20% larger fuel tanks for West of England duties, but GWR says that the '800s' are being modified to match as they will now spend more time running on diesel power than expected.

As a result, the main difference between the two designs will be the larger roof-mounted braking resistors of the '802s', which are raised slightly to lift them away from seawater pooling in the roof well during high tides along the Dawlish sea wall section. This modification to the design is a response to the electronics problems suffered by CrossCountry Class 220/221 DEMUs on this route during bad weather.

Main line testing of the pre-series GWR Class 802s began in Somerset in August 2017. Internally, the trains are similar to the Government-sponsored Class 800s, with identical seating and interior layout. GWR says '802' diagrams will include duties to Bristol, South Wales and the Cotswold Line, as well as Devon and Cornwall, but '800s' are unlikely to venture west, except on the busiest summer weekends.

Replacement GWR seating moquette is due to be fitted on the '802s' when they arrive in the UK, although the trains retain the very firm seats that have been the cause of much adverse comment since the Class 800s entered traffic last October.

GWR Class 802

Operator:	Great Western Railway
Built:	2018-19
Introduced:	July 2018
No. ordered:	See separate panel
No. of cars per train:	Five/nine
Numbers:	See separate panel
Capacity:	326/655 seats
Order value:	£361m
Routes:	Paddington-Paignton/ Plymouth/Penzance
Power supply:	25kv AC overhead/3x or 5x940hp MTU diesel
Max speed:	125mph (140mph design speed)
Formation:	See separate panel
Features:	Air-conditioning, fast-acting sliding doors, gangways within set, wi-fi, at-seat charging points, bi-mode electric/diesel
Owner/finance:	Eversholt Rail Leasing

porterbrook

Pistoia assembles Class 802 bodyshells from flatpack kits of aluminium extrusions shipped in from Hitachi plants in Japan. This is in contrast to the company's Newton Aycliffe factory, which fits out pre-assembled and painted bodyshells before forming them into complete trains. BEN JONES

TPE Class 802/2

Operator:	TransPennine Express
Built:	2018-19
Introduced:	2019
No. ordered:	19 (95 vehicles)
No. of cars per train:	Five
Numbers:	802201-219
Order value:	TBC
Routes:	Manchester-Leeds-Newcastle-Edinburgh
Power supply:	25kv AC overhead/3x940hp MTU diesel
Max speed:	125mph (140mph design speed)
Formation:	See separate panel
Capacity:	342 seats
Features:	Air-conditioning, fast-acting sliding doors, gangways within set, wi-fi, at-seat entertainment
Owner/finance:	Angel Trains

TRANSPENNINE AT300S

Two further orders have been placed for AT300s by British operators, totalling 120 vehicles. Both TransPennine Express and Hull Trains are part of the FirstGroup empire and, taking advantage of GWR's order, the two TOCs serving northern England will receive similar 24 five-car Class 802 sets from Hitachi. Eversholt Rail Leasing has provided funding for the GWR order, while the TPE and Hull Trains sets are being financed by Angel Trains.

TPE has 19 Class 802/2s on order, while Hull Trains will replace its current Class 180 fleet with five five-car Class 802/3s in 2019. In total, Hitachi will build 1285 Class 800-802 vehicles at its plants in Japan, Newton Aycliffe in County Durham and Pistoia in Italy between 2015 and 2019.

Hitachi originally expected to complete at least some of the Class 802/2s and 802/3s bi-mode trains at Newton Aycliffe, but it confirmed in May that seven of the 24 trains will be built in Japan, and the other 17 will be assembled in Italy and delivered by rail to the UK.

The first of TPE's 19 five-car trains was delivered by sea to Southampton Docks on June 11.

During its two-month journey it crossed the Atlantic and Pacific oceans, as well as passing through the Panama Canal.

Production began in Japan in December 2017 and the fleet is due to start testing in the UK from summer 2018 with a view to entering service from summer 2019.

The '802/2s', marketed as 'Nova 1' by TPE, will be part of a much-improved and expanded inter-city fleet for the franchise. An extra 13 million seats per year will be provided across TPE routes, on more 'upmarket' inter-city trains.

The '802/2s' will be employed on TPE routes across the north of England and via the East Coast Main Line to Newcastle and Edinburgh, where they will be able to run at up to 125mph, with a possible increase to 140mph when the infrastructure allows it.

Although the final scope of Network Rail's Trans-Pennine electrification scheme is still uncertain, the route is scheduled for a major upgrade over the next few years, possibly featuring discontinuous electrification over the steepest sections. However, the bi-mode trains will be able to take advantage of 25kv AC power between Liverpool and Stalybridge, through Leeds and between Colton Junction, south of York and Edinburgh.

The trains will provide 161 more seats than the existing Class 185 DMUs on this busy inter-city route. Passengers will benefit from more spacious carriages, extra legroom and additional luggage space and the on-board experience

The first two Class 802/2s for TransPennine Express (TPE) were built in Japan and the first set arrived in the UK for testing in June. After its epic journey across the Pacific and Atlantic oceans, one of the driving cars is unloaded at Southampton Docks. HITACHI RAIL EUROPE

porterbrook

Hull Trains has five AT300s on order for Hull-King's Cross open access services. They are due to enter service in 2019. HULL TRAINS

A First Class saloon of a GWR Class 802. The seats are identical to the DfT-procured Intercity Express Trains, which have been the subject of some criticism from users since their introduction. GWR plans to re-cover the seats with new moquette before they enter public service. BEN JONES

Hull Trains Class 802/3

Operator:	Hull Trains
Built:	2018-19
Introduced:	2019
No. ordered:	Five (25 vehicles)
No. of cars per train:	Five
Numbers:	802301-305
Order value:	£60m
Routes:	Hull-King's Cross
Power supply:	25kv AC overhead/ 3x940hp MTU diesel
Max speed:	125mph (140mph design speed)
Capacity:	327 seats
Features:	Air-conditioning, fast-acting sliding doors, gangways within set, wi-fi
Owner/finance:	Angel Trains

will be completely transformed.

Each new train will offer free wi-fi in both Standard and First Class, as well as a complimentary on-board entertainment system, Exstream, allowing customers to stream the latest movies and TV shows during their journey.

They will be based at Hitachi's £80m depot in Doncaster and also maintained at Edinburgh Craigentinny with servicing at Edge Hill in Liverpool, Heaton in Newcastle and at York. TPE's investment is also supporting thousands of jobs across the UK through Hitachi's decision to choose over 30 UK firms to supply key components. Businesses chosen include Lucchini Unipart Rail (LUR), whose Manchester factory will build wheelsets for the

trains. The fleet will also support long-term jobs at depots along the route, including Hitachi's £80m depot in Doncaster.

Modern MTU diesel power packs supplied by Rolls-Royce will cut harmful emissions under diesel power by up to 90%.

OPEN ACCESS

In November 2016, FirstGroup-owned open access operator Hull Trains announced that it was procuring five five-car AT300 sets to replace the Alstom Class 180 diesel multiple units it currently uses on the Hull-King's Cross route. They will be largely similar to the TPE Class 802/2s and will also be based at Hitachi's Doncaster 'mothership', but with servicing also taking place in Hull and at Bounds Green in London.

The £60m investment in high-tech Hitachi

trains will deliver 20% extra capacity per train and 50% overall, additional services, enhanced interiors and the potential for faster speeds once the infrastructure allows it. Each Class 802/2 set will have 327 seats providing greater comfort than existing trains, as well as more environmentally friendly operation using 25kv AC electric power as soon as they join the East Coast Main Line at Temple Hirst Junction, between Selby and Doncaster. Diesel power will only be required on the non-electrified section from Temple Hirst to Hull, but will also be useful during disruption on the ECML when diversions are required.

The order followed Hull Trains' recent success in securing a track access extension from the Office of Rail and Road (ORR), guaranteeing Hull Trains direct services to and from London until 2029.

INTER-CITY

After more than 40 years of HST operation, GWR's Paddington terminus in London is changing rapidly. As the nine-car Class 800/3 Intercity Express Trains and West of England Class 802s enter service, scenes such as this view of a pair of '800s' arriving from the west on June 22, 2018 will become the norm in 2019. PAUL SMITH

porterbrook

CLASS 397: TRANSPENNINE'S NEW ANGLO-SCOTTISH EMUs

One of three new train fleets ordered by TransPennine Express at a cost of £500 million, these Spanish-built 125mph EMUs will provide a step up in quality from the existing trains employed on TPE's routes from northern England to Edinburgh and Glasgow.

One of several recent UK orders for the Spanish rolling stock manufacturer Construcciones y Auxiliar de Ferrocarriles (CAF), Class 397 is one of three new inter-city fleets set to transform TransPennine Express operations in 2018/19.

Nicknamed 'Nova 2' by TPE, the trains are 25kv AC overhead electric multiple units (EMUs) built to replace TPE's existing Siemens Class 350/4s on the inter-city route between north-west England and Scotland. As well as the existing Manchester Airport-Glasgow/Edinburgh route, they will allow TPE to introduce a new service between Liverpool and Scotland. A total of 12 five-car units are currently under construction in northern Spain and are due to enter service in spring 2019.

The EMUs were ordered by FirstGroup after it was confirmed that it had secured the TransPennine Express franchise in April 2016. A month later,

the 'Nova 2' order was confirmed in parallel with orders for 13 locomotive-hauled Mk 5a sets (Nova 3) from CAF and 19 AT300 bi-mode 125mph trains from Hitachi Rail Europe. No UK manufacturer took part in the competitive tender process.

Construction of the Class 397s was well under way at CAF's factory in Beasain, northern Spain, in the summer of 2018 and the first set is expected to be delivered to the UK in October. The first set was completed in early June and after initial static and low speed testing at the factory it moved to the VUZ Velim test centre in the Czech Republic for a more extensive test programme. A second set was due to join it at Velim in July, allowing testing while working in multiple with two pantographs raised, coupling and uncoupling procedures and ensuring the electrical footprint of the trains is within the agreed parameters. Testing at a dedicated facility such as Velim allows much of the electrical testing and acceptance work to be completed without

disrupting main line operations in the UK.

CAF will also undertake dynamic testing of the 'Nova 2' sets on high-speed standard gauge lines in Spain, which share the same 25kv AC overhead electric supply as UK main lines. These tests will also allow CAF to undertake the agreed mileage accumulation and fault-free running required before the trains are accepted by the leasing company and operator.

Testing in the UK will take place towards the end of 2018 on the West Coast Main Line – most likely on the northern end of the route, which offers an ideal mix of high-speed sections, challenging climbs and unpredictable weather conditions.

Funded by Eversholt Rail Leasing, they will replace four-car Class 350/4s (which will be cascaded to London Northwestern Railway). The '397s' will be maintained by Alstom at Longsight in Manchester and Polmadie in Glasgow.

"Once ready, these futuristic trains will be some of the most modern in the country, and I'm thrilled to be overseeing such an important transformation," said TPE managing director Leo Goodwin when the '397s' were ordered.

José María Muguruza, project manager for CAF, added: "The trains are the 'high

porterbrook

An artist's impression of the new Class 397 'Nova 2' EMUs being built by CAF in Spain for TransPennine Express. The trains will run at up to 125mph and replace TPE's current Class 350/4 EMUs on services from the north-west of England to Glasgow and Edinburgh. TPE

CAF Class 397

Operator:	TransPennine Express
Built:	2018-19
Introduced:	May 2019
No. ordered:	12
No. of cars per train:	Five (60 vehicles)
Numbers:	397001-012
Order value:	£230m (includes Mk 5a sets)
Routes:	Liverpool/Manchester-Glasgow/Edinburgh
Power supply:	25kv AC overhead
Max speed:	125mph
Power rating:	TBC
Formation:	DM+TS+MS+TS+DM
Capacity:	290 seats
Features:	Air-conditioning, wi-fi, CCTV, electronic seat reservations, at-seat entertainment
Owner/finance:	Eversholt Rail Leasing

speed' variant of our 'Civity' electric train, are capable of 125mph operation, and will provide passengers with a new journey experience."

These 'Civity' units are formed of five cars each and will feature a modern functional interior design, equipped with passenger information systems and on-board wi-fi servers aim to maximise passenger comfort.

In addition, the design of the new trains is expected to reduce track damage thanks to their lighter weight. Energy consumption is also reduced thanks to their regenerative braking system. CAF will provide technical support and spares for both fleets. Maintenance will be undertaken by Alstom at its facilities at Longsight (Manchester), Edge Hill (Liverpool) and Polmadie (Glasgow).

Other standard equipment on the Class 397s includes Automatic Warning System (AWS) and Train Protection Warning System (TPWS), air-conditioning, CCTV, on-train monitoring and recording, an electronic seat reservation system and a fire detection system.

The three new train fleets will provide an extra 13m seats a year, which is enough to fill Manchester United's Old Trafford stadium more than 150 times.

Mr Goodwin said: "This will enable us to transform the customer experience over the life of our franchise and our three new train fleets will form a key part of this improvement.

"Whether travelling to work, for business or leisure, our services are going to offer more seats, improved connectivity and a higher standard of comfort.

"The on-board experience will be second-to-none and we will provide customers with a real alternative to the car and congested road network."

Investment in new fleets will mean every train operated by TPE will have free wi-fi and media servers allowing customers to stream TV shows, films and entertainment, advanced on-board customer information, modern interior with spacious seating, air-conditioning and power sockets at every seat.

The first completed Class 397 EMU was delivered from Spain to the VUZ Velim facility in the Czech Republic for dynamic testing at the beginning of July. On July 3, the five-car train made its first high-speed runs on the centre's large and small test rings, which allow speeds of up to 200kph (125mph). Testing was due to continue throughout the summer prior to the delivery of the first '397s' to the UK.
QUINTUS VOSMAN

CAF Mk 5a

Operator:	TransPennine Express
Built:	2017-18
Introduced:	October 2018
No. ordered:	13
No. of cars per train:	Five (66 vehicles)
Order value:	£110m
Routes:	Liverpool-Newcastle (later Manchester-Scarborough/ Middlesbrough)
Power supply:	Diesel-powered (Class 68)
Max speed:	100mph
Power rating:	N/A
Formation:	DTSO+BSO+ TSO+TSO+FO
Capacity:	291 seats (plus six tip-up seats)
Features:	Air-conditioning, wi-fi, CCTV, electronic seat reservations, at-seat entertainment
Owner/finance:	Beacon Rail Leasing

The first TransPennine Express Mk 5a 'Nova 3' set on test at the VUZ Velim test centre in the Czech Republic in April. The fixed five-coach sets should start work on the Liverpool-Newcastle route in October.
KEITH FENDER

ransPennine Express (TPE) has three new train fleets on order, nicknamed 'Nova 1' to 'Nova 3'. The first to be introduced, starting the countdown to the operator's transformation of inter-city and inter-regional services across the north of England, will be 'Nova 3' in the autumn of 2018.

Ordered from CAF in Spain, these 13 new five-car locomotive-powered trains were something of a novelty for a railway dominated by multiple units. They will be powered by Vossloh/Stadler Class 68 diesels sub-leased from Direct Rail Services (DRS). In the longer-term, should electrification become more widespread across TPE routes, the '68s' could – in theory – be replaced by electric locomotives with relative ease. Locomotive-hauled trains also offer the potential for adding additional capacity easily by inserting extra vehicles if required.

However, in the first instance, these new sets of coaching stock will replace TPE Class 185 three-car DMUs, bringing a high-quality inter-city ambience, new features and extra seating capacity on key routes across the north of England. The coaches will initially be used between Liverpool, Manchester, Huddersfield, Leeds, York, Scarborough and Newcastle. From 2019 they will also run to Middlesbrough. They will initially operate at up to 100mph, but have the capability to run at 125mph as routes are upgraded and electrified.

INTER-CITY QUALITY

Designated as Mk 5a stock, the 66 vehicles are related to the Mk 5s also being built by CAF for Caledonian Sleeper (see page 60). However, they differ in many respects, including body length and width, the provision of standard buffers and interior equipment. Along with the sleeper vehicles, they are the first locomotive-hauled coaches to be ordered by a British operator since the BR Mk 4s introduced in 1988-91.

They will be formed into 13 five-coach trains, with one spare driving trailer vehicle, composed of one First Class vehicle, two Standard Class opens, a Brake Standard class car and a Standard Class driving trailer. Construction is shared between CAF's plants in Beasain (intermediate coaches) and Irun (driving trailers), both in northern Spain.

The contract also includes maintenance of the new trains. CAF's commitment to the Mk 5a fleet will continue until the end of the TPE franchise with the provision of technical support service for maintenance, and integral spares management.

Each set has 291 seats, with power sockets at every pair of seats, free wi-fi, real-time travel information and an on-board media server streaming television programmes and films. An electronic seat reservation system will show whether a seat is free, occupied, or reserved for part of the journey.

Production started in October 2016 and in March 2018 the first completed rake was sent for testing at the VUZ Velim test track in the Czech Republic. Two modified Class 68s, Nos. 68019/021, were sent from the UK via Cuxhaven and by rail across Germany to work with the set. However, due to delays in transporting the '68s', the initial dynamic tests took place with a Siemens 'Vectron' electric locomotive.

porterbrook

'NOVA 3':
INTER-CITY QUALITY FOR TPE'S DIESEL ROUTES

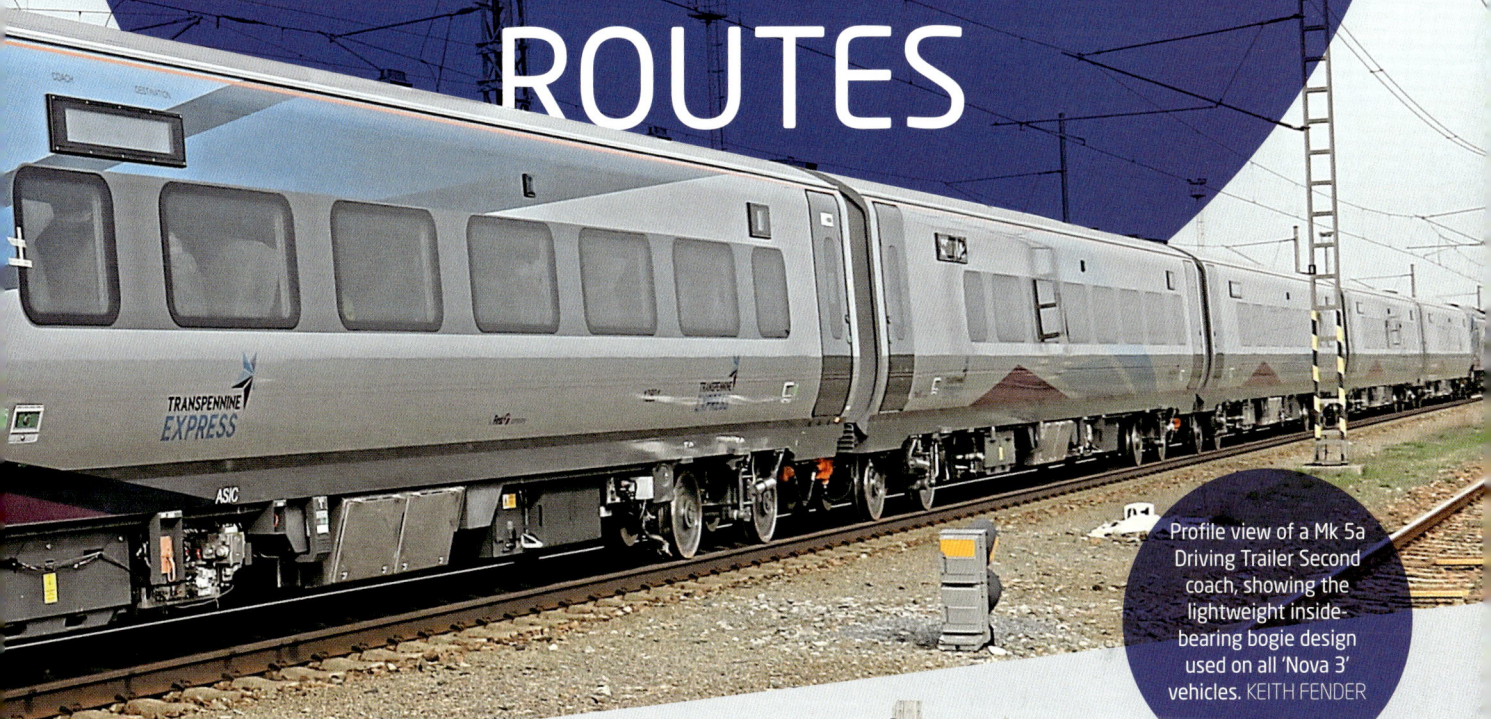

Profile view of a Mk 5a Driving Trailer Second coach, showing the lightweight inside-bearing bogie design used on all 'Nova 3' vehicles. KEITH FENDER

Left: Mk 5a Standard Open No. 12703 on test at Velim. Note the wide, sealed gangways between vehicles improving access through the train and reducing interior noise compared to older locomotive-hauled stock. KEITH FENDER

Left: Prior to moving to Velim for testing with the Mk 5a set, reliveried No. 68021 *Tireless* stands inside the maintenance shed at the DRS Crewe Gresty Lane depot. Thanks to new visibility rules for British trains, the TPE '68s' are the first locomotives for many years without the previously mandatory yellow warning panels on each end. TPE

Above: After completion, the first 'Nova 3' set was transferred by rail from the Spanish/French border to the Czech Republic. On March 18, 2018 the stylish new train makes an unusual sight running along the Elbe Valley between Dresden and the Czech border. QUINTUS VOSMAN

(DAS) and European Rail Traffic Management System (ERTMS) equipment, which will be required as part of Network Rail's planned Trans-Pennine route upgrade over the next few years. The York-Leeds-Manchester route will be one of the first main lines to undergo conversion to European Train Control System (ETCS) as part of NR's Digital Railway strategy.

TECHNICAL SPECIFICATIONS

The Mk 5a vehicles are 2.7m wide but of two different lengths; the outer TF and DT cars being 22.37m long and the intermediate TS cars slightly shorter at 22.2m. The total set length is 111.4m, or 131.85m including the locomotive. All vehicles feature standard drawhooks and couplings, inside-frame bogies, axle-mounted disc brakes, wheelslide protection and sanding equipment fitted on the third axle of the Driving Trailer.

The wide, single-leaf plug doors are fitted with obstacle detecting sensors and can be selectively opened used GPS-based Automatic Selective Door Opening (ASDO), relayed via track-mounted balises if required. An automatic passenger counting system is also fitted, with separate totals recorded for each coach and updated after each station stop.

The Trailer First vehicle will be semi-permanently coupled to a locomotive and only has a gangway at one end. It also features a small food preparation area and galley for

Type testing at Velim included aerodynamics, brake systems and passenger information systems – all of which could be undertaken in a controlled environment without requiring access to already congested main lines in the UK.

The 13 trains will be allocated to 12 daily diagrams with one set in reserve or undergoing maintenance. DRS is hiring 16 Class 68s to TPE to power the trains (Nos. 68019-034), each of which will be modified with remote door controls, CCTV, Mk 5a train management system, passenger alarm interface/intercom and electronic destination displays, as well as receiving TPE's latest silver/blue livery.

Standard features on the Mk 5a fleet include air-conditioning, fire and smoke detectors, a 'black box' event recorder, CCTV, Driver Advisory System

porterbrook

Above: TPE is sub-leasing 16 Class 68s from DRS to power the 'Nova 3' sets, each of which is receiving modifications for their new passenger role. On April 12, No. 68021 powers around the test circuit at Velim in the Czech Republic, pushing a set of Mk 5a vehicles. KEITH FENDER

First Class at-seat service, 30 seats in 2+1 bays with tables and an accessible toilet. The two Trailer Standard vehicles seat 69 passengers each in 2+2 formation with both bays and airline-style seating and both have a standard toilet cubicle. The third Standard Class intermediate coach has 59 seats, a standard toilet cubicle and a multi-purpose area with six tip-up seats

TPE's parent company, FirstGroup, undertook competitive tending for the supply of the rolling stock and separate financing. The order is financed by Beacon Rail, which also owns the Class 68 diesel locomotives that will power the trains. Maintenance will be undertaken by Alstom at Longsight in Manchester and Edge Hill in Liverpool.

No UK manufacturers took

> By July 2018 the first 'Nova 3' sets had arrived in northern England. Assuming testing and acceptance trials go to plan, the first sets will enter service with TPE in autumn 2018.

that can be used for stowing bicycles and luggage. Finally, the Driving Trailer has 64 Standard Class seats, no toilet and two luggage spaces.

Every pair of seats has a standard three-pin power socket and USB charging points between the two seat bases. First Class seats will have leather upholstery in a similar style to the refurbished Class 185s, while Standard Class passengers have fabric upholstered Fainsa seats, similar to those in the Hitachi Class 800-802 bi-mode trains.

part in the tender won by CAF, as Bombardier's Derby plant is at capacity building 'Aventra' EMUs and Hitachi's Newton Aycliffe site is busy supplying the Intercity Express Programme and ScotRail Class 385 fleets.

By July 2018, the first 'Nova 3' sets had arrived in northern England, having been delivered by sea from Spain to Portbury Docks in Bristol. Testing running and acceptance trials will be underway by the time you read this, hopefully allowing TPE to introduce the trains as planned in the autumn.

porterbrook

The new Mk 5 vehicles will bring a significant improvement in quality and facilities for Caledonian Sleeper passengers. This is a computer-generated image of one of the wheelchair-accessible suites. CALEDONIAN SLEEPER

HOTEL QUALITY
FOR SCOTTISH SLEEPERS

The Scottish Government is funding a £100 million transformation of overnight services between London and Scotland's biggest cities, with new trains promising a high-quality hotel ambience.

In 2015, the Caledonian Sleeper service, operated as part of the ScotRail franchise since privatisation in the mid-1990s, was split into a separate operation, with Serco as the new franchisee. As part of the franchise agreement, Serco committed to procuring new rolling stock to replace the existing fleet of ex-BR Mk 2 and Mk 3 coaches.

In February 2015, Serco signed a £150m deal with Construcciones y Auxiliar de Ferrocarriles (CAF) of Spain for 75 Mk 5 coaches of five different types. Finance has been arranged by the

The first batch of five Mk 5 vehicles arrived in the UK in January 2018 after tests in the Czech Republic. Having travelled across Europe by rail, they were delivered to Scotland by rail for further tests. KEITH FENDER

porterbrook

CAF Mk 5

Operator:	Caledonian Sleeper
Built:	2016-18
Introduced:	October 2018
No. ordered:	75
No. of cars per train:	Eight
Order value:	£150m
Routes:	London-Glasgow/ Edinburgh/Aberdeen/ Inverness/Fort William
Power supply:	Locomotive-hauled
Max speed:	100mph
Power rating:	N/A
Features:	Air-conditioning, wi-fi, seated cars, bar car, luxury sleeper suites, showers
Owner/finance:	Caledonian Sleepers Rail Leasing Ltd

Mark 5 sleepers pay their first visit to the West Highland Line behind No. 73971 on a test run from Polmadie to Arrochar and back on April 10, 2018. The outward trip is captured between Craigendoran and Helensburgh Upper. The coaches are incomplete internally and have yet to receive their external logos. The bogies are wired up to computer equipment within. RAILWAY MAGAZINE ARCHIVE

porterbrook

Above: A view of the club car, showing the mix of seating booths and individual bar-style seats. Sleeper passengers will be able to enjoy a drink and a meal before retiring to their room or reclining seat. CALEDONIAN SLEEPER

Caledonian Sleepers Rail Leasing Ltd subsidiary of Lombard North Central plc, supported by a £60m capital grant from the Scottish Government.

The order comprises 40 sleeping cars with six en suite luxury cabins and four cabins without en suite facilities (Nos. 15301-340), 14 accessible sleeping cars with two fully accessible cabins (one with a double bed and one with a foldable upper bed), two cabins with en suite facilities, showers and double beds and two cabins with foldable upper berths, plus two shower rooms (Nos. 15201-14), 10 club cars with bar and lounge (Nos. 15101-110) and 11 seated cars with brake accommodation (Nos. 15001-011).

They will be formed into four 16-coach trains (comprising two eight-coach portions), with 11 spares vehicles for Scottish Government-supported overnight trains between London Euston and Glasgow/Edinburgh, Aberdeen, Inverness and Fort William.

They will be the first new locomotive-hauled passenger coaches on the British network since the BR Mk 4 InterCity 225 sets in 1989-92.

Each eight-coach set features First and Second Class cars with reclining seats, a 'brasserie'-style club car and sleeper cars with high-quality hotel-style en suite cabins. The First Class cars have airline-style 'pod' flat-bed seats for greater passenger comfort. One other major advantage of the new trains is that they are designed to be much more accessible than the ones they are replacing, with Persons of Restricted Mobility (PRM)-compliant accessible cabins and facilities.

Edinburgh-based designer Ian Smith has created a 'contemporary' interior style for the coaches. The new carriages feature double-room accommodation, a first for the UK. The new fleet will also have en suite toilets and showers in a number of rooms in the accommodation carriages. Other features include en suite berths and double rooms for couples, hotel-style key cards, telephone and gadget-charging facilities and on-board wi-fi. Caledonian Sleeper has also committed to ending

> The new fleet will have en suite toilets and showers in a number of rooms, plus double rooms for couples, hotel-style key card entry, gadget charging facilities and on-board wi-fi.

the practice of double occupancy in sleeper cabins when the new trains are introduced.

The first trains are expected to enter service on the London-Glasgow/Edinburgh 'Lowlander' route in October. Once all four trains are available they will operate in a similar fashion to the current trains, with full eight-coach sets working between London, Edinburgh, Glasgow

porterbrook

Top right: Classic room: Once the new trains are in service, Caledonian Sleeper will end the unpopular practice of sharing cabins. CALEDONIAN SLEEPER

Bottom right: Travellers will have the option of a seated coach fitted with reclining seats or airline-style 'pods' that will lay flat for sleeping. CALEDONIAN SLEEPER

and Inverness, a four-coach short set handling the Fort William portion and a six-coach set operating to Aberdeen six nights a week.

Caledonian Sleeper plans to offer Comfort Seats starting from £45, Classic Rooms (twin or single) from £85 per person, Club Rooms (en suite twin or single) from £125 per person and Suites (double bed with en suite) from £200 per person.

TESTING, TESTING

The Mk 5 fleet is being built at CAF's Beasain factory in northern Spain. The first five vehicles moved to the Czech Republic for testing in August 2017, travelling by rail across Europe from Hendaye on the Spanish border to the VUZ Velim test centre near Prague. Externally complete but with no interiors, they underwent extensive dynamic testing before being delivered to Polmadie depot in Glasgow in January 2018.

On a visit to see the new trains being built, Scottish Transport Minister Humza Yousaf MSP said: "When investing upwards of £60m, we wanted a new Sleeper service that incorporated cutting-edge design, top-class passenger catering and a service that was emblematic of the very best Scotland

has to offer. We also wanted a service that would enhance travel options to and from London, as well as encourage more tourists to visit Scotland."

Describing the Mk 5s as "breath-taking", he said they offered a "glimpse of what innovative and never-before-seen upgrades to services rail passengers can expect".

Peter Strachan, Serco chairman for UK Rail, added: "To design, build and introduce a new fleet of sleeper coaches is extremely challenging and complex.

"We still have a lot of work to do to successfully bring the new sleeper fleet into service, but I am really excited about the quality of experience we will be able to offer our guests when it arrives."

MODERNISED LOCOMOTIVES

Traction for Caledonian Sleeper services will continue to be supplied by GB Railfreight, using refurbished Class 92 electric locomotives originally built for Channel Tunnel services to haul the London to Edinburgh/Glasgow trunk legs. Extensively rebuilt Class 73/9 electro-diesels will be used singly to Fort William and Aberdeen, with pairs on the heavier and more challenging Inverness

leg. As the Mk 5 stock uses Dellner auto-couplers rather than conventional buffers and couplings, GBRf has invested in retractable auto-couplers for its dedicated sleeper locomotives. Both the '92s' and the '73s' were modified by Wabtec-Brush in Loughborough during 2017/18, ready to start work with the new stock. It was originally planned to send examples of each type to the Czech Republic for testing with the stock at Velim. This did not occur, but main line testing started in Scotland and on the West Coast Main Line in late Spring and was ongoing as this publication went to press.

One interesting development that may be possible after the introduction of the Mk 5s is the revival of internal Scottish overnight services using spare Mk 3 sleepers and Mk 2 seated vehicles. To improve links between Edinburgh, the far north and Orkney, the Scottish Government is investigating the possibility of an Edinburgh-Inverness-Wick/Thurso sleeper, connecting via a bus link with ferries to and from Orkney. The service would require substantial support from the Scottish Government to make it viable, but could also be used to transport lightweight, high-value freight and parcels to maximise its value to remote communities.

REGIO REVOLU

Spanish train-builder CAF has scored a number of successes over the last two years, securing contracts for regional DMU fleets for Arriva Northern, West Midlands Railway and, most recently, Transport for Wales (pictured). Many of these trains will be built in Wales, at CAF's new £30 million factory near Newport, which is due to open later this year. TRANSPORT FOR WALES

porterbrook

NAL TION

Rail travel in and around Britain's big cities has been one of the major success stories of the last decades, but overcrowded and unreliable trains have been a source of frustration for passengers. Billions of pounds are now being invested to replace and expand train fleets across Wales, Scotland and the English regions to cater for rising demand now and over the coming decade.

porterbrook

CIVITY PROMISES BETTER QUALITY FOR NORTHERN ROUTES

The first four-car Class 331 set for Arriva Rail North on test at the VUZ Velim test track in the Czech Republic in April 2018. The first sets should enter service with Northern in December. QUINTUS VOSMAN

porterbrook

CAF Class 331 EMU

Operator:	Arriva Rail North
Built:	2017-19
Introduced:	December 2018-December 2019
No. ordered:	43 (31xthree-car, 12xfour-car)
No. of cars per train:	Three/four
Numbers:	331001-031 (three-car), 331101-112 (four-car)
Order value:	£492m (includes Class 195s)
Routes:	West Yorkshire and Greater Manchester electric networks, plus Manchester-Preston-Blackpool
Power supply:	25kv AC overhead
Max Speed:	100mph
Power rating:	1760kW
Formation:	DMSL+PTS+DMS (331/0), DMSL+PTS+TS+DMS (331/1)
Capacity:	203 seats (331/0), 283 seats (331/1)
Features:	Air-conditioning, CCTV, wi-fi, at-seat power points, electronic seat reservation displays, passenger counting system
Owner/finance:	Eversholt Rail Leasing

T he Northern franchise, covering regional services across the north of England, encompasses a diverse range of operations, from intensive suburban services to rural branch lines and busy inter-urban routes. As such it operates an equally diverse train fleet, much of which dates from the 1980s. One of the priorities of the new Northern franchise, awarded to Deutsche Bahn subsidiary Arriva in December 2015, was the replacement of the unpopular Class 142/144 'Pacer' railbuses, which operate commuter and regional services in Yorkshire, the north-west and the north-east of England. The Department of Transport (DfT) made their replacement with new or refurbished trains a condition of the franchise. Arriva's solution was a large fleet of 98 new electric and diesel trains, ordered from Construcciones y Auxiliar de Ferrocarriles (CAF) of Spain.

Financed by Eversholt Rail Leasing, the fleet of 'Civity UK' multiple units consists of 55 Class 195 DMUs (25 two-car and 30 three-car) and 43 Class 331 EMUs (31 three-car and 12 four-car), totalling 281 vehicles.

Class 195 and Class 331 bodyshells are being constructed at CAF's plant in Zaragoza. They are then transferred to the company's site in Irún, close to the French border, for final assembly and pairing with bogies and wheelsets produced in Beasain.

Designed for 100mph operation, both the '195s' and 331 EMUs have central driving seats, are equipped with Dellner auto couplers and both feature pre-installed CAF-manufactured ERTMS equipment.

However, that is unlikely to be commissioned for use for several years, as only a few main routes across the north are likely to be upgraded with digital in-cab signalling over the next 15 years.

The interiors are common to both fleets, incorporating Fainsa seats and specially designed seat cushion and fabric and tables or seat back drop-down tables at all seats.

Both variants have lightweight aluminium bodies, air-conditioning throughout, supplied by Merak of Madrid, Dellner auto-couplers at the outer ends and bar couplings within the set. Both powered and unpowered bogies have a 2250mm wheelbase and the distance between bogie pivots is 16m. Lightweight inside-bearing bogies are fitted, with disc brakes acting on the outer faces of all wheels.

Pneumatic braking and sanding equipment is by Knorr-Bremse. Standard British AWS, Train

Class 331 vehicles on the assembly line at CAF's factory in Zaragoza on January 31, 2018. The Spanish plant is building 281 vehicles for Northern. KEITH FENDER

The first complete four-car Class 331/1, No. 331101, in the test house in Zaragoza on January 31, 2018. These four-car sets will replace ex-BR Class 321/322 EMUs in West Yorkshire. KEITH FENDER

porterbrook

Three-car DMU No. 195101 was sent by CAF for dynamic testing in the Czech Republic and is also expected to visit Romania for testing at the Faurei test centre. On its long journey across Europe, the DMU was spotted in the Czech Republic being hauled by a former Czechoslovakian diesel owned by open access freight operator CZ Logistics. QUINTUS VOSMAN

Protection Warning System (TPWS) and On-Train Monitoring & Recording (OTMR) is fitted, along with CAF's own ERTMS in-cab signalling equipment.

Each car has two pairs of double-leaf sliding plug doors manufactured by Knorr-Bremse subsidiary IFE. Driver access is by a separate door on each side of the cab.

Electronic seat reservation indicators as well as power sockets are provided. Free on-board wi-fi will be offered to all passengers.

The £492 million order for the combined fleet of 281 vehicles was placed by Eversholt in January 2016, and options exist to order additional vehicles. Both fleets will be delivered by sea from northern Spain, and will allow the cascade or withdrawal of existing units to begin at the end of 2018.

DIESEL CIVITY

All Class 195 driving vehicles will be equipped with an MTU power pack incorporating a 390kW Euro IIIB-compliant Daimler engine and a ZF Ecolife Rail hydro-mechanical transmission driving both axles of the powered bogie.

The driving cars are 24m long, 2.71m wide and 3.87m high above the railhead. A two-car Class 195/0 is 48m long over the couplings, while a three-car Class 195/1 is 71.4m long, including a slightly shorter Trailer Standard (TS) vehicle at 23.4m. The Driving Motor Second Lavatory (DMSL) car features a wheelchair-accessible toilet manufactured by Alte. The Driving Motor Second (DMS) vehicle is very similar but does not have a toilet cubicle. A two-car set seats 123, while a three-car '195/1' with intermediate Trailer Second (TS) vehicle has 203 seats arranged

Above: The striking and attractive cab-front design of the Class 195s and 331s will bring a modern look to routes across the north of England from December, and provide a strong contrast with the old ex-BR trains they will replace. KEITH FENDER

in a 2+2 formation with no provision for First Class. According to CAF's figures, a Class 195/0 weighs 87 tonnes and a Class 195/1 is 123 tonnes.

Construction started in July 2017 and the trains will be phased into service between December 2018 and December 2019. Northern plans to introduce the Class 195s between Chester and Leeds from December 2018, as approval is anticipated following dynamic testing at Velim in the Czech Republic, Romania and the UK during the second half of the year. The first Class 195 set arrived in the UK in late-June and was due to be joined by a second set soon afterwards.

The Class 195s will be based at Newton Heath depot in Manchester and a new £42m maintenance and servicing facility is planned for the former Springs Branch depot site in Wigan. Although full details of where the Class 195s will be deployed are yet to be revealed, they are likely to be introduced on Arriva Rail North's 'Northern Connect' network of key inter-urban routes linking the major cities of the north. Their introduction will allow older DMUs to be cascaded to other duties, which in turn will allow the operator to withdraw all 102 'Pacer' railbuses before the end of 2019.

porterbrook

ELECTRIC VARIANT

While the promised electrification of more key routes across northern England looks to have stalled, Northern still operates several important electrified suburban networks serving Greater Manchester, the north-west and West Yorkshire. To allow an increase in capacity and quality on these routes, 43 Class 331 EMUs will be introduced between December 2018 and December 2019. Of these, 31 will be three-car Class 331/0s and 12 will be four-car Class 331/1s. An option remains for a fifth car to be added to the '331/1s' if demand is sufficient.

The '331/1s' will replace ex-BR Class 321 and 322 EMUs on the Aire Valley (Leeds-Bradford/Skipton/Ilkley) and Leeds-Doncaster 'stoppers' supported by West Yorkshire Passenger Transport Executive (WYPTE) in 2019, working alongside refurbished Class 333 EMUs that were also built by CAF.

Three-car Class 331/0s will be deployed on electrified services from Manchester Airport to Blackpool via Bolton and Preston, which should be available for electric operation from November 2018, and on Manchester Piccadilly-Hadfield/Glossop, Manchester-Crewe, Macclesfield and Stoke suburban services, where they will replace Class 323s dating from the early-1990s.

The first complete four-car Class 331 was unveiled in Zaragoza in January 2018. It underwent various static and low speed tests at the CAF factory before moving to Velim in the Czech Republic for dynamic testing of braking, electronics and electrical equipment. The set will then transfer to northern England in the summer for testing and approval runs on the Network Rail system prior to an expected entry into passenger service in December.

Northern plans to introduce the trains on its busiest routes serving Manchester from early-2019. The EMUs will be based at Allerton depot near Liverpool, with those based east of the Pennines likely to be maintained at Neville Hill depot in Leeds.

Each three-car Class 331 set is formed of two driving motor vehicles, which are equipped with traction converters (one per driving car), 220kW asynchronous traction motors supplied by Austrian manufacturer Traktionsysteme Austria (TSA), and an unpowered intermediate car fitted with an ABB traction transformer and Brecknell Willis pantograph. The fourth car in a Class 331/1 is an unpowered Trailer Second. Traction power control systems are supplied by CAF's Power and Automation division.

The driving cars are 24.03m long, 2.71m wide and 3.87m high above the railhead. A three-car Class 331/0 is 71.4m long over the couplings and weighs in at 125.5 tonnes, while a four-car Class 331/1 is 94.75m long and weighs 157.4 tonnes. The Driving Motor Second Lavatory (DMSL) car features a wheelchair-accessible toilet manufactured by Alte. The Driving Motor Second (DMS) vehicle is very similar but does not have a toilet cubicle. A three-car set seats 203, while a four-car '331/1' has 283 seats arranged in a 2+2 formation with no provision for First Class.

Inset: An artist's impression of the Class 195 DMU, which will allow Northern to withdraw all 102 Class 142/144 diesel railbuses by the end of 2019. CAF

Below: The first Class 195 DMU arrived in the UK by sea from northern Spain in late-June. A driving car from No. 195001 is unloaded on to the quayside at Royal Portbury Docks, near Bristol, on June 25. ARRIVA RAIL NORTH

CAF Class 195 DMU

Operator:	Arriva Rail North
Built:	2017-19
Introduced:	December 2018-December 2019
No. ordered:	55 (25xtwo-car, 30xthree-car)
No. of cars per train:	Two/three
Numbers:	195001-025 (two-car), 195101-130 (three-car)
Order value:	£492m (includes Class 331s)
Routes:	Various across northern England
Power supply:	1xDaimler 390kW diesel per car
Max speed:	100mph
Formation:	DMSL+DMS (195/0), DMSL+TS+DMS (195/1)
Capacity:	123 seats (195/0), 203 seats (195/1)
Features:	Air-conditioning, CCTV, wi-fi, at-seat power points, electronic seat reservation displays, passenger counting system
Owner/finance:	Eversholt Rail Leasing

West Midlands Railway has 26 'Civity UK' DMUs on order from CAF. They should enter service in the second half of 2020, replacing ex-BR Class 150s and Class 170 'Turbostars' that will be cascaded to other parts of the country. CAF

EXTRA DIESEL TRAINS FOR WEST MIDLANDS COMMUTER LINES

After winning large orders from Northern and TransPennine Express, CAF's successful run continues with this new diesel fleet for Abellio's West Midlands Railway operation.

When the West Midlands franchise changed hands in December 2017, the Abellio/JR East/Mitsui joint venture unveiled two major orders totalling 107 new trains. As well as selecting Bombardier's 'Aventra' EMU to boost West Coast Main Line semi-fast services and replace Birmingham's Cross-City Line fleet, it opted to update its diesel fleet with 26 'Civity UK' DMUs from Construcciones y Auxiliar de Ferrocarriles (CAF) of Spain.

This fleet of 12 two and 14 four-car DMUs from CAF's 'Civity' family will be known as Class 196 and will share similarities with other CAF diesel units being built for Arriva Rail North and Transport for Wales. The trains are intended to replace West Midlands Railway's Class 170 'Turbostars' in the second half of 2020, and supplement the newer fleet of Class 172 suburban 'Turbostar' derivatives on cross-city diesel routes through Birmingham Snow Hill to Stratford-upon-Avon, Solihull, Kidderminster and Worcester and from Birmingham New Street to Hereford and Shrewsbury.

The new Class 196s will have additional capacity in comparison to existing WMT fleets, but they have been designed to offer improved seat pitch and window views in all positions, in response to recent passenger complaints about seats on many new trains.

Passengers will have access to a USB charging point or a plug socket, and every seat in standard or priority positions will have either a seat-back or fixed table. The cantilever design of the seats will make cleaning easier and provide extra space for luggage.

BUILT IN WALES?

The £177 million trains will contribute towards increasing the size of the WMR fleet by 25% by

porterbrook

the end of the franchise in 2026. CAF will not only manufacture the trains, but will provide maintenance for the duration of the franchise. It has not yet indicated where the trains will be built, but assembly could take place at its new assembly facility near Newport in South Wales, which is due to open later this year.

In addition to the new CAF trains, WMR will receive eight two-car Class 172 DMUs displaced from London Overground's Gospel Oak-Barking route from October 2018. It will also become the first operator of Vivarail's Class 230 'D-Train' in late-2018, when three two-car diesel sets take over from Class 150 DMUs on the Bedford-Bletchley route (see page 106).

The '196s' will be based at Tyseley depot in Birmingham, alongside the Class 172s, with servicing also taking place at various other locations. Their delivery will allow WMR to simplify its diesel fleet, reducing it from four classes (Classes 150, 153, 170 and 172) to just two basic types, plus the Class 230s outbased at Bletchley.

> The £177m Class 196s, formed of 12 two-car and 14 four-car trains, will contribute towards a 25% increase in the size of the West Midlands Railway fleet by the time the franchise ends in 2026.

CAF Class 196 DMU

Operator:	Abellio/JR East West Midlands Railway
Built:	2019-20
Introduced:	2020
No. ordered:	26 (12xtwo-car, 14xfour-car)
No. of cars per train:	Two/four (80 vehicles)
Numbers:	TBC
Order value:	£177m
Routes:	Birmingham-Hereford/Stratford/Shrewsbury
Power supply:	TBC 1x diesel motor per car
Max speed:	100mph
Formation:	DMSL+DMS (two-car), TBC (four-car)
Capacity:	TBC
Features:	Air-conditioning, wi-fi, at-seat charging points, passenger information systems, through gangways
Owner/finance:	Infracapital/Deutsche Asset Management

The '196s' will join WMR's existing Bombardier Class 172s on local and inter-urban services in the West Midlands, replacing older Class 170s that will be cascaded to other operators. No. 172219 calls at Henley in Arden with a London Midland service from Birmingham to Stratford-upon-Avon on April 26, 2013. FRASER PITHIE

porterbrook

An artist's impression of how Greater Anglia's new bi-mode regional trains will look when they enter service in 2019.
GREATER ANGLIA

STADLER PROMISES
SWISS PRECISION FOR GREATER ANGLIA

Swiss train-builder Stadler Rail has burst on to the UK rail scene by winning four high-profile contracts in recent months, the largest of which is a £900 million order for FLIRT bi-mode regional trains and inter-city EMUs for Abellio Greater Anglia.

How did a small family company specialising in bespoke trains for narrow gauge and mountain railways become one of the fastest growing and most innovative train builders in Europe in less than 20 years?

In a world dominated by the three global giants – Alstom, Bombardier and Siemens – Stadler Rail has become a serious player, competing for major orders from incumbent national operators, but also taking advantage of the trends towards regionalisation and open access operation to win smaller orders for its railcars, LRVs and multiple units.

In the mid-1990s Stadler employed only around 100 people, but since the turn of the century it has grown rapidly – today the total is more than 7000 employees in 13 countries worldwide, producing hundreds of rail vehicles, trams, locomotives and coaches per year, managing maintenance contracts, refurbishment programmes and supporting operators across Europe, the US and Australia.

Like any successful company, Stadler has taken advantage of changing market conditions, but it has also benefitted from being in the right place at the right time, capitalising on dissatisfaction with the 'big three' to win large orders.

Alstom, Bombardier and Siemens have all experienced lengthy delays in recent years, both in the design and construction of new trains and in getting them approved for use on European railways – most notably in Germany. However, Stadler prides itself on having never missed a delivery deadline and on being able to deliver new trains at short notice when required.

The company places great faith in its ability to deliver trains that work reliably 'out of the box' – something that will be vital if Stadler is to meet the ambitious target of having its first FLIRT UK trains running in the UK in 2019.

Greater Anglia has ordered 378 vehicles, being

porterbrook

Stadler Class 745

Operator:	Greater Anglia
Built:	2017-19
Introduced:	2019
No. ordered:	20 (240 vehicles)
No. of cars per train:	12
Numbers:	745001-010 (inter-city), 745101-110 (Stansted Express)
Order value:	£600m (total)
Routes:	Liverpool Street-Norwich/Stansted Airport
Power supply:	25kv AC overhead
Max speed:	100mph
Power rating:	5.2MW
Length:	236m
Seating capacity:	757 (745/0), 767 (745/1)
Features:	Air-conditioning, wi-fi, USB and standard charging points, passenger information system, retractable steps, low floor design for easy access
Owner/finance:	Rock Rail

Stadler Class 755

Operator:	Greater Anglia
Built:	2017-19
Introduced:	2019
No. ordered:	38 (138 vehicles)
No. of cars per train:	Three/four
Numbers:	755301-314 (three-car), 755401-424 (four-car)
Order value:	£600m (total)
Routes:	East Anglia regional routes/branches
Power supply:	25kv AC overhead/diesel bi-mode
Max speed:	100mph
Power rating:	Class 755/3: 2.6MW (25kv AC)/1.92MW (diesel), Class 755/4: 2.6MW (25kv AC)/960kW (diesel)
Length:	Class 755/3: 65m, Class 755/4: 80.7m
Seating capacity:	167 (755/3), 229 (755/4)
Features:	Air-conditioning, wi-fi, USB and standard charging points, passenger information system, retractable steps, low floor design for easy access
Owner/finance:	Rock Rail

The first completed Class 755/4 electro-diesel FLIRT in the test hall at Bussnang in Switzerland on May 3. This unit will go to Romania for testing before delivery to the UK in October. CHRIS MILNER

assembled at Stadler plants in Switzerland, Poland and Hungary to the UK loading gauge and formed into 20 12-car inter-city/Stansted Express 25kv AC electric sets, 24 four-car and 14 three-car electro-diesel regional units. This £610m order was Stadler's first for main line trains in the UK, part of a £1.54 billion total fleet replacement programme by GA franchise holder Abellio. Stadler will also maintain the new trains at Crown Point depot in Norwich.

The whole basis of the procurement of the new Anglia fleet is to have it in place before the new Persons of Restricted Mobility (PRM) regulations come into force on January 1, 2020, so deliveries of production sets will start in spring 2019 and all 58 trains will be in service by the end of the year.

They are financed by Rock Rail East Anglia, a joint venture between Rock Rail, Aberdeen Standard Investments and GLIL Infrastructure,

Left: First Class interior of the Class 745/0 inter-city FLIRT for the London-Norwich route.
GREATER ANGLIA

Right: Standard Class FLIRT interior showing the flip-up seats providing extra capacity at busy times.
GREATER ANGLIA

and will be leased to Abellio Greater Anglia.

STRONG REPUTATION

Stadler is well known for delivering reliable trains – it is proud of the Swiss quality it delivers to customers. It uses high-quality materials for its interiors, mechanical and electrical components, designed to deliver lower life-cycle costs because the trains are built to be more reliable.

While they may still be an unknown quantity to British rail users, if Greater Anglia's FLIRTs live up to the high standards of quality and reliability set by Stadler trains elsewhere in Europe, they could set a new benchmark for British passenger trains.

Abellio's £1.6bn total fleet replacement programme is split between Bombardier Derby and Stadler, with the Swiss firm supplying a variant of its hugely successful FLIRT articulated train in both electric and bi-mode form. More than 1500 FLIRTs have been sold to 18 countries across mainland Europe and beyond for suburban, regional and inter-city use, and in electric, multi-voltage, diesel and electro-diesel variants.

Of the 20 Class 745 inter-city trains, 10 will replace Class 90 and Mk 3 locomotive-hauled sets on the Liverpool Street-Norwich route and 10 will replace Class 379s to provide an improved Stansted Express service. The main differences between the two sub-classes will be the absence of First Class accommodation and a catering area on the Stansted sets.

The Class 755s will take over rural and regional routes including Norwich to Sheringham, Lowestoft, Great Yarmouth and Cambridge; Ipswich to Felixstowe, Lowestoft, Cambridge and Peterborough and Marks Tey to Sudbury from late-2019. The Class 153 and 170 DMUs they replace will be cascaded to Transport for Wales and the recently refurbished Class 156s are likely to join their sisters operating for Northern or the East Midlands franchise.

A 12-car Class 745 formation showing the mix of articulated and bogie vehicles. The Class 745s are effectively two six-car half-sets coupled back-to-back.
GREATER ANGLIA

The Stadler trains will offer more seats, free wi-fi, power and USB charging points, air-conditioning and accessible toilets (two per train in the 12-car sets and one in each regional set). They will also have cycle spaces and large picture windows and will be the centrepiece of many other improvements across the franchise, including more frequent services, faster journeys and more capacity, with 55% more seats into London in the morning peak.

A novel feature of the GA FLIRTs is the higher than usual number of tip-up seats to give extra seating capacity at busy times. The inter-city 12-car sets will have no fewer than 53, while the airport sets have 45. The Class 755/3s and 755/4s have 23 and 27 respectively.

The seating capacity of the Class 745/0 inter-city sets will be around 25% greater than the current trains – 757 compared to 534, or 618 on a nine-coach Mk 3 set. First Class seating will be in 2+1 format with tables and seats lined up with the windows wherever possible, both in bays and airline-style.

INTERNATIONAL EFFORT

Although Stadler's main assembly facilities

porterbrook

Top: Aluminium bodyshells for Greater Anglia FLIRTs being assembled at Bussnang in Switzerland on May 3. Assembly of the British trains will be shared across Stadler factories in Switzerland, Hungary and Poland. CHRIS MILNER

Middle: The Class 755s feature a centrally positioned power pack fitted with either two or four Deutz V8 diesel engines, which provide power to the traction motors when running away from the electrified network. Passengers and crew will be able to pass through this section using a gangway between the engines. CHRIS MILNER

Bottom: Greater Anglia FLIRT vehicles in the assembly hall at Bussnang alongside closely related trains being built for Swiss operators. CHRIS MILNER

are in Switzerland, at Bussnang and Erlen near Zurich, the construction of the GA fleet will be a truly international effort across the company's plants in Spain (Valencia), Szolnok in Hungary and Siedlce in Poland.

Bussnang is assembling the first three Class 755s using bodyshells manufactured in Hungary and painted in Poland, and the bogies are being manufactured in Winterthur, which produces all FLIRT bogies. Aluminium bodyshells for the rest of the '755' fleet are being assembled in Szolnok then shipped to Poland for painting, fitting out, final assembly and commissioning. However, the first eight power packs have been produced at Bussnang and the rest will come from the former Vossloh plant in Valencia, which also built the DRS Class 68s. This will allow Bussnang to focus on constructing the 20 Class 745s, which are due to enter service in late-2019. Commissioning of all 58 trains will take place at Erlen before the trains are delivered to the UK.

Testing will involve up to 10 pre-series trains at seven locations in Switzerland, Germany and test centres at Velim in the Czech Republic and Faurei in Romania during the second half of 2018. The first set to be completed, bi-mode No. 755401, will go to Faurei before delivery to the UK for acceptance and commissioning in October. Four Stansted Class 745/1s are due to arrive first, followed by the 10 Class 745/0s and then the rest of the Stansted sets. This will allow GA to withdraw its non-compliant Mk 3 trains from the Norwich route before the December 2019 PRM-TSI deadline.

POWER PACK

The Class 755 diesel power pack, positioned in the centre of the trains, meets the latest tighter standards for emissions and is also quieter than existing diesel-powered trains. Three-car Class 755/3s have two Deutz 480kW (645hp) 16-cylinder V8 engines while the four-car '755/4s' are considerably more powerful with four Deutz V8 engines installed in the power pack providing 1.92MW – around 2600hp. Power is fed to the electric traction package, giving rapid acceleration and smoother operation than with hydraulic or mechanical transmissions.

The power pack is designed for conversion in the future to alternative power sources, either diesel to battery or hydrogen, into tri-mode form or removal altogether to create a straight electric train.

As with many other modern electric trains, energy created when braking under 25kv AC power

is returned to the overhead wires via regenerative braking, saving further energy and lowering operating costs. Even in diesel mode, the trains can brake electrically using brake resistors, which reduces wear and tear on braking systems.

Ralf Warwel, marketing director of Stadler for UK, said: "The bi-mode trains for East Anglia will enable a flexible, comfortable and interruption-free operation on the whole network, reducing exhaust emissions, vibrations and fuel consumption whenever electrification is available."

Stadler and Greater Anglia spent many months in consultation with stakeholders, passenger groups and staff to devise the optimum design and layout for the trains.

Mike Kean, franchise and programmes director at Greater Anglia, said: "Our priority for the new trains was to involve the public and stakeholders fully in the design process and we are pleased that this extensive consultation process has resulted in so much useful feedback which will inform and shape the final design."

porterbrook

CLASS 385:
EMUs FOR SCOTLAND'S BUSIEST COMMUTER ROUTES

Over the last decade ScotRail's passenger numbers have increased by more than 30%. Unreliable and ageing diesel trains and poor punctuality have been exacerbated by overcrowding on key routes, particularly across the Central Belt of the country. To cope with the extra demand, the ScotRail Alliance, formed by Network Rail and Abellio ScotRail, is in the process of electrifying various key routes, including the primary Edinburgh-Glasgow line via Falkirk High, the secondary route via Shotts and from both of Scotland's two largest cities to Stirling, Alloa and Dunblane.

To work these lines, supplement the existing EMU fleet on other routes and release diesel units to increase capacity elsewhere or for cascade to other operators, Abellio ScotRail ordered 70 new electric trains immediately after securing the franchise in October 2014. Hitachi Rail Europe was selected to build the new fleet, using its AT200 regional train concept. The first trains were completed in Japan in 2016 and delivered to the UK for pre-series testing.

The original plan was for them to enter service on the Edinburgh Waverley-Glasgow Queen Street route in December 2016, but neither the upgraded infrastructure nor the trains were ready in time. Instead, a partial electric service started with ScotRail Class 380s sharing duties with Class 170 DMUs in January 2018. Unfortunately, the Class 385s experienced a number of teething troubles that prevented their introduction as planned, including transformer and software issues and an unexpected by-product of the external design. During driver training it was discovered that the curved windscreens caused drivers to see multiple reflected signals in certain lighting conditions. Several months elapsed while a solution was found, which involved designing and fitting new windscreens.

This delay had knock-on effects for both ScotRail and other operators expecting to receive cascaded Class 170s for the May timetable change. As a further interim measure, ScotRail organised the short-term lease of 10 Class 365 EMUs recently released by Great Northern.

Just as these units were entering service on the Edinburgh-Glasgow route in late-June, the modified Class 385s were approved for passenger service by the Office of Road and Rail's (ORR) chief inspector of railways. This paved the way for driver training to recommence, ready for the first '385s' to start work in July. Initially, they are to be used in limited numbers to release Class 170s, but over the remainder of 2018 they are expected to gradually allow the Class 380s to return to their normal duties and replace the borrowed Class 365s. When eight-car Class 385s are introduced on the Edinburgh-Glasgow via Falkirk High route in 2019, they will improve capacity by up to 44% at peak times, compared to a six-car Class 170 DMU.

However, before this can happen, Network Rail must complete the rebuilding of Glasgow Queen Street station and various platforms at other locations, including Edinburgh Waverley, to accommodate longer trains.

As sufficient trains become available, they will gradually be phased-in on a mix of inter-urban

Set 'T2', one of seven pre-series sets built in Japan and delivered to the UK early for testing and approvals work, stands on the dockside at Teesport near Middlesbrough. Class 385 bodyshells are delivered by sea to this location and forwarded by road for fitting out at Newton Aycliffe. HITACHI RAIL EUROPE

porterbrook

Hitachi Class 385

Operator:	Abellio ScotRail
Built:	2016-18
Introduced:	July 2018
No. ordered:	70 (234 vehicles)
No. of cars per train:	Three/four
Numbers:	385001-046 (three-car), 385101-124 (four-car)
Order value:	£475m
Routes:	Edinburgh-Glasgow via Falkirk High or Shotts, Edinburgh/ Glasgow-Dunblane/ Alloa, Cathcart Circle (Glasgow), North Berwick and Glasgow-Carstairs
Power supply:	25kv AC overhead
Max speed:	100mph
Power rating:	4x Hitachi asynchronous traction motors of 250kW each
Formation:	DMSO+PTSO+DMSO (385/0), DMCO+ PTSO+TSO+DMSO (385/1)
Seating capacity:	206 (385/0), 273 (385/1)
Features:	Air-conditioning, wi-fi, passenger information system, at-seat charging points, through gangways
Owner/finance:	Caledonian Rail Leasing

BUILT IN THE NORTH EAST

CLASS 385 | HITACHI Inspire the Next

385 103

Most of the Class 385 fleet is being built at Hitachi Rail Europe's Newton Aycliffe plant in County Durham. On October 10, 2017, four completed sets were rolled out for the press and stakeholders. BEN JONES

porterbrook

suburban routes, starting with Edinburgh-North Berwick and the Cathcart Circle, Neilston and Lanark/Carstairs suburban lines south of Glasgow (three-car sets). Once electrification of the Stirling-Dunblane/Alloa lines and Edinburgh-Glasgow via Shotts lines is completed in 2019 they will take over from DMUs on these busy routes. Class 385s are also expected to work the recently-electrified Glasgow-Falkirk Grahamston via Cumbernauld route from 2019.

While most of the existing ScotRail fleet will be retained and refurbished or cascaded elsewhere, the operator's oldest electric trains, the Class 314s, dating from 1979, will be retired and are likely to be scrapped.

JAPANESE TECHNOLOGY

The £475 million order covers the construction of 234 EMU vehicles (70 trains), divided into 46 three-car Class 385/0s and 24 four-car Class 385/1s. As well as having an extra car, the '385/1s' differ from their sisters in having a small 20-seat First Class compartment in one driving car. Although much of the Scottish network is Standard Class only, First Class is retained on ScotRail's main inter-city routes and the key Edinburgh Waverley-Glasgow Queen Street service.

The bulk of the new fleet will be constructed at Hitachi Rail Europe's factory in Newton Aycliffe, County Durham, but the first seven units were built at Hitachi's Kasado factory in Japan. Construction of the first sets began in November 2015 and the first trains were delivered to Scotland in December 2016.

If Transport Scotland exercises an option to extend the Abellio contract from seven to 10 years in 2020, a further 10 three-car Class 385s could be purchased. These units would enter service in 2023.

From a passenger point of view, the new electric trains should offer an improved experience with more seats, a quieter journey, free wi-fi, at-seat charging points, extra cycle spaces and a fully accessible toilet in every set. A multi-purpose space is also provided to accommodate bulky luggage, prams and standing passengers at busy times, while electronic destination and information displays on the train ends, sides and inside each car will keep passengers updated.

A passenger counting system will record people entering and leaving the train, allowing the ScotRail Alliance to better match capacity with demand.

According to ScotRail, the new trains are around 18% more energy efficient than the diesel trains they are replacing, as well as being much quieter and cleaner, especially in stations where CO_2 emissions from trains will be significantly reduced.

Regenerative braking will also convert kinetic energy of the train into electrical energy that is then fed back into the overhead line power supply system during braking. The trains also use LED lighting technology and have a 'sleep mode' to make them more energy efficient.

The Class 385s will be able to operate in three, four, six, seven and, eventually, eight-car formations, providing much more flexibility to match demand with capacity. Unlike the existing Class 170s, the '385s' have through gangways between all cars so that every part of the train can be accessed from the inside.

Since the similarly equipped Class 380s were introduced on the 'E&G' route in January, ScotRail has noticed an upswing in ticket sales, a reduction in fare dodging and increased sales on catering

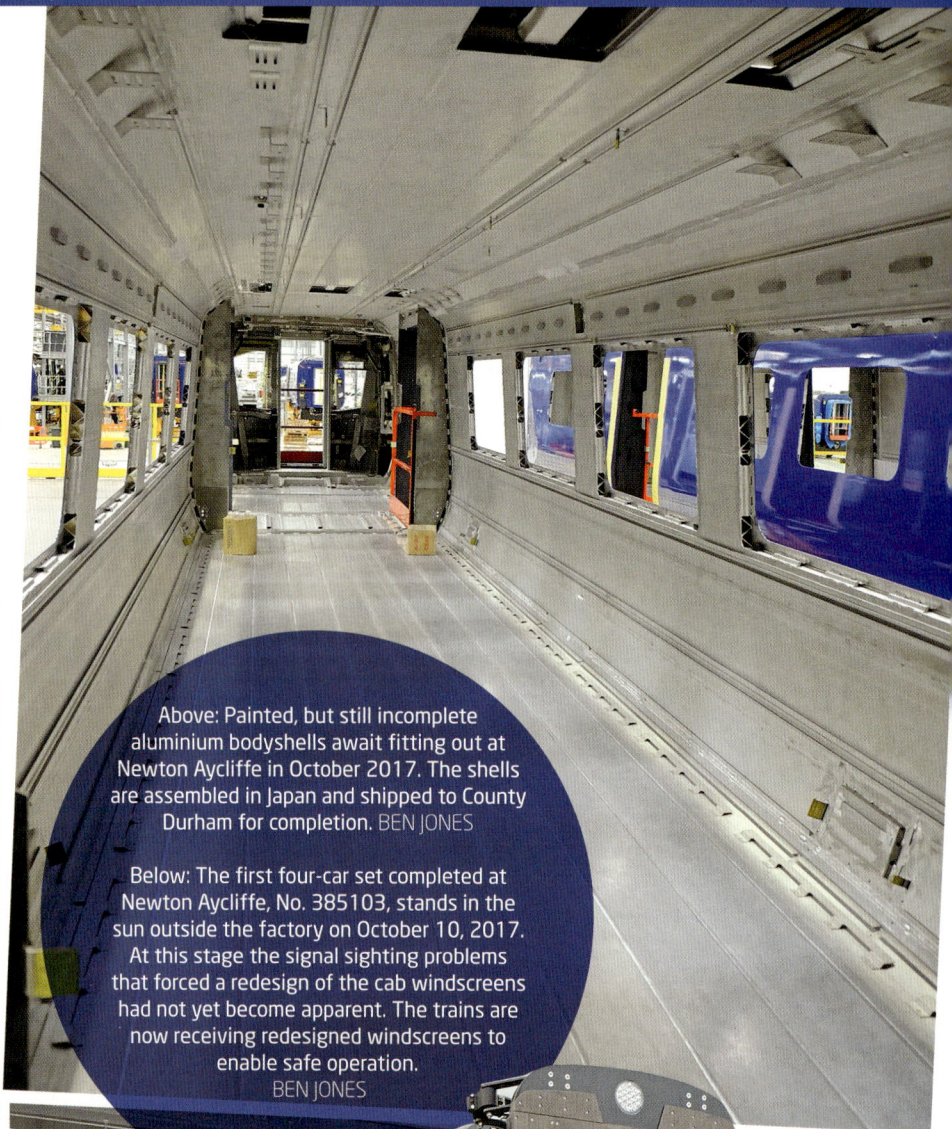

Above: Painted, but still incomplete aluminium bodyshells await fitting out at Newton Aycliffe in October 2017. The shells are assembled in Japan and shipped to County Durham for completion. BEN JONES

Below: The first four-car set completed at Newton Aycliffe, No. 385103, stands in the sun outside the factory on October 10, 2017. At this stage the signal sighting problems that forced a redesign of the cab windscreens had not yet become apparent. The trains are now receiving redesigned windscreens to enable safe operation. BEN JONES

porterbrook

Right: A completed four-car Class 385/1 at Newton Aycliffe. After many months of delays, the class was finally cleared for passenger operation on the Edinburgh Waverley-Glasgow Queen Street route in late-June 2018 and started work on a limited number of diagrams in July. HITACHI RAIL EUROPE

trolleys that can now reach every passenger on the train.

Two wheelchair spaces are provided per set, along with an accessible toilet that features a new 'assist' facility to allow companion access to the cubicle while maintaining privacy. The trains are fully compliant with the latest TSI PRM (technical specification for inter-operability for persons with reduced mobility), which come into force on January 1, 2020.

MAINTENANCE

Hitachi Rail Europe established a base for operations in Glasgow in April 2015, allowing it to work closely with Abellio in the delivery of the Class 385 trains. The contract between them includes a 10-year maintenance deal and the trains will be maintained by Hitachi at Craigentinny depot in Edinburgh. They will also be serviced at several other locations, including Millerhill on the outskirts of Edinburgh and Eastfield in Glasgow. Abellio and Hitachi have committed to increasing reliability and lowering 'whole life' costs through continuous improvement work streams and greater use of remote monitoring techniques.

Above: Unusually, a four-car Class 385 was sent to Germany in 2017 for dynamic tests at DB Systemtechnik's Minden test centre. Unable to work under its own power on the Deutsche Bahn network, the instrumented set was towed by a DB Class 120 electric at speeds of up to 100mph to test how it behaved at higher speeds. BRIAN DANIELS

Below: Highlighting the impressive scale of Hitachi's Newton Aycliffe operation, a large number of Class 385 vehicles make their way along the assembly line on October 10, 2017. BEN JONES

porterbrook

Stadler's bespoke metro solution for Merseyside

Swiss train-builder Stadler is supplying a specially-designed fleet of new metro-style EMUs for the Merseyrail electric network that serves Liverpool and its surrounding areas.

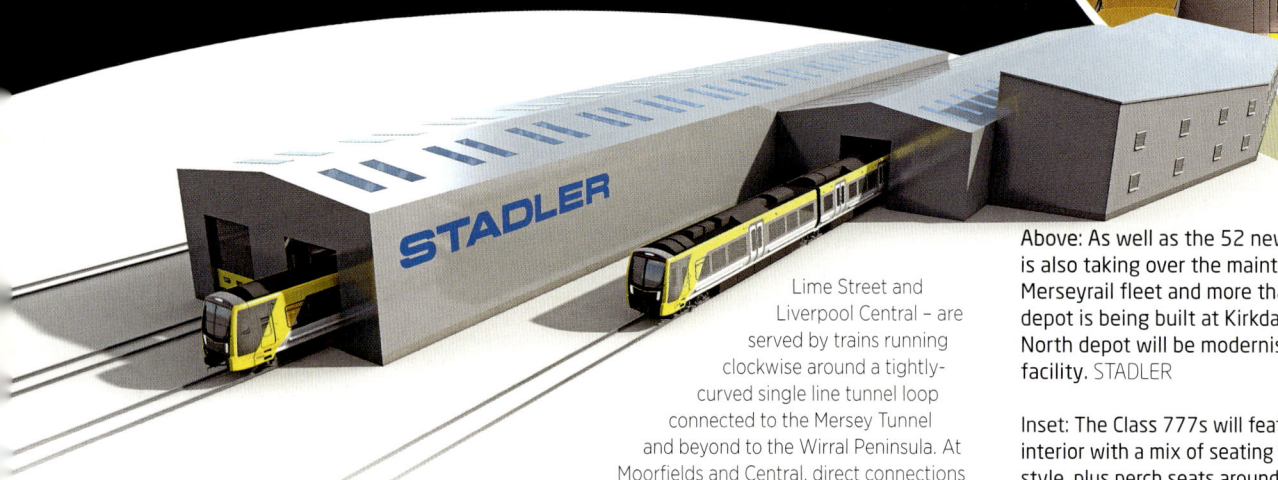

Above: As well as the 52 new trains, Stadler is also taking over the maintenance of the Merseyrail fleet and more than 150 staff. A new depot is being built at Kirkdale and Birkenhead North depot will be modernised as a stabling facility. STADLER

Inset: The Class 777s will feature a bright, modern interior with a mix of seating in bays and airline-style, plus perch seats around doors and extensive standing areas. Other features will include intelligent lighting and air-conditioning, at-seat charging and USB sockets, step-free access and wide gangways. STADLER

T he Merseyside suburban network was one of the first electric railway systems in Britain, with the Mersey Railway going over to electric operation on May 3, 1903. Trains ran every three minutes under the River Mersey from Liverpool Central to Birkenhead Hamilton Square in a much cleaner environment than the steam trains used previously.

Today, Merseyrail operates a dedicated network of electrified local railways linking Liverpool with Southport, Ormskirk, Hunt's Cross, the Wirral Peninsula and Chester via Birkenhead. It currently operates one of the oldest passenger fleets in the country, formed of ex-BR Class 507 and 508 three-car EMUs built in 1978-80.

Unlike much of the rest of the British main line network, Merseyrail is not a franchised operation – it is operated as a concession from local transport authority Merseytravel by a 50:50 joint venture between Netherlands Railways subsidiary Abellio and Serco.

Together, they operate one of the most punctual and reliable rail networks in the UK, running almost 800 trains per day serving 67 stations, four of which are underground in Liverpool city centre.

Those stations – James Street, Moorfields,

Lime Street and Liverpool Central – are served by trains running clockwise around a tightly-curved single line tunnel loop connected to the Mersey Tunnel and beyond to the Wirral Peninsula. At Moorfields and Central, direct connections are made with the Northern Line, which links Southport and Ormskirk in the north with Hunt's Cross to the south of the city.

Restricted tunnels, tight curves and short platforms mean that Merseyrail trains need to have a relatively small profile. When Merseytravel put the contract for new rolling stock out to tender, the winning bid came from Stadler, which offered a bespoke solution, rather than a variant of an existing product line.

SHORTLIST

The subject of replacing the ageing Class 507 and Class 508 fleet was raised by Merseytravel as early as in 2011, although it wasn't until the following year that work started in earnest. In January 2016 five rolling stock manufacturers were shortlisted to build the new fleet; Bombardier, Siemens, CAF, Stadler and a consortium of Mitsui/Alstom/East Japan Railway Company.

In December 2016, a £460 million deal was signed with Stadler (£700m including a 35-year maintenance agreement) to build and maintain 52 metro trains for the Liverpool City Region from 2020. Merseytravel also has an option for a further 60 vehicles (15 sets) to increase capacity if necessary.

The project is being financed from a fund established for the purpose by Merseytravel,

as well as loans from sources including the European Investment Bank. Merseytravel will own the trains and lease them to the operating concessionaire, which will be paid a lower operating fee to account for the expected increase in revenue and lower running costs.

The fleet renewal programme also includes power supply, track, station upgrades and refurbishment of the Kirkdale and Birkenhead North depots. The reduced journey times and better reliability will allow 52 new EMUs to replace the current fleet of 59 trains.

They will have lower floors than the current trains, at 960mm above rail level and they will provide fully step-free access for all passengers, making Merseyrail the most accessible traditional network in the UK. A new maintenance depot at Kirkdale will be entirely designed and built by BAM Nuttall and operated by Stadler. The Swiss company is to transfer 155 maintenance staff from Merseyrail into its own operations, bringing the total number of employees in the UK to more than 200 people by 2019.

Stadler's executive vice president and head

porterbrook

Stadler
Class 777

Operator:	Merseyrail
Built:	2018-20
Introduced:	2019-21
No. ordered:	52
No. of cars per train:	Four (208 vehicles)
Numbers:	777001-052
Order value:	£460m (£700m including maintenance)
Routes:	Merseyrail third-rail network
Power supply:	750v DC third-rail
Max speed:	75mph
Power rating:	2800hp
Formation:	DMSO+MSO+MSO+DMSO
Capacity:	182 seats, 302 standing
Features:	Regenerative braking, hybrid battery option, passenger information systems, step-free access, 'smart' lighting features
Owner/finance:	Merseytravel

A computer-generated image of Merseyrail's new Class 777 metro trains, the first of which will arrive on Merseyside in the summer of 2019. The articulated four-car trains are a bespoke metro design tailored to the specific requirements of the Merseyrail system. STADLER

of marketing & sales, Peter Jenelten, said: "This contract with Merseytravel marks a very important milestone for Stadler in the UK. It will bring safer, more comfortable trains that can carry more people and will help provide the Liverpool City Region with the metro service it deserves."

The '777s' will be able to carry 60% more passengers than the Class 507s and 508s, although they have the same number of seats. They will be entirely walk-through, increasing capacity to 486 (182 seated, 302 standing, and two wheelchair users).

They will feature an articulated four-car design with significantly increased overall capacity and faster acceleration and deceleration. A combination of reduced weight (99 tonnes, representing a 5.5-tonne weight reduction) and more efficient electrical systems will give a 20% reduction in energy use.

The Class 777 fleet will be in service by 2021, with the first unit arriving for testing by the middle of 2019. Lightweight articulated cars, assembled from aluminium extrusions, are designed to make the '777s' safer and more energy efficient than the trains they replace.

At 64.98m-long and 2.82m-wide the fleet will operate on 750v DC third-rail supply at a maximum speed of 75mph. All sets will be equipped with batteries to allow independent movement within depots.

Merseyrail's Long-Term Rail Strategy states that the Class 777s will be involved in a trial of dual-voltage operation in 2020 to allow for future network expansions to destinations such as Warrington, Skelmersdale and Wrexham. Stadler has designed the '777s' with the ability to be retrofitted for 25kv AC and ETCS Level II operation.

INNOVATIONS

The new vehicles have been designed for the specific needs of customers travelling on the Merseyrail network, with many features reflecting what passengers said they wanted in a Transport Focus survey in 2013.

Safety features will include intelligent sliding steps that, combined with infrastructure improvements, will virtually eliminate gaps between platforms and trains, providing step-free access at all entrances. With no 'gap to mind', the new fleet will be highly accessible for all, from wheelchair users and the elderly, to cyclists and passengers with luggage. Sensitive door sensors will detect obstructions, while 'intelligent' door illuminations will inform passengers when it is safe to board and alight.

On-board safety will be enhanced by open saloons with no gangway doors, as well as CCTV and a glazed cabin for the driver. The trains will also have wider aisles, larger vestibules, perch seats and more grab handles, making them safer for the larger number of standing passengers. The Merseyrail network has a number of tunnels that makes delivering reliable wi-fi more challenging. However, there will be plug sockets and USB charging points available at every seat.

All interior fittings will be damage resistant and the exterior will be graffiti and spray paint resistant.

Stadler says the driving cab offers "a comfortable working environment with enhanced sight lines, an ergonomic desk arrangement and all of the functionality required for flexible, modern trains".

Despite criticism and industrial action by train crews over the proposal of redeploying guards into other roles after the Class 507 and 508 units are withdrawn, the Class 777 units have been designed to operate in Driver Controlled Operation (DCO) mode.

ASSEMBLY UNDERWAY

Construction of the first trains started at Stadler's plant in Szolnok, Hungary in June 2018. The design work was completed over the summer and the first components started to be produced. Design work was also underway on the exterior and technical aspects of the train at Stadler's Valencia plant in Spain.

Over the second half of 2018, the aluminium car bodies were due to be machined, welded, assembled, sandblasted and given corrosion protection prior to being painted.

Around half of the vehicles will move to Stadler's bespoke vehicles facility at Altenrhein in Switzerland for final assembly, with the other half due to move to Siedlce in Poland. The first completed bodyshell is scheduled to be delivered in September and the first completed train will arrive on Merseyside for testing in the summer of 2019. The series fleet should all be in service by the end of 2020. A revised timetable will be introduced in 2021 once the existing Class 507 and 508 units have been withdrawn.

Transport for Wales
£5bn masterplan to transform rail network

June 2018 saw the Welsh Government unveil a £5 billion masterplan to replace every passenger train in the country over the next six years and transform rail services on commuter, regional and rural routes.

Rail services across Wales will be transformed over the next six years as the Welsh Government and its development partner KeolisAmey invest around £5 billion in a complete fleet replacement, new stations, electrification and the creation of a higher frequency 'metro' network centred on Cardiff.

Every train in Wales will be replaced as part of an £800m programme, with 50% of the new fleet to be built at CAF's new £30m factory near Newport. Almost 150 new trains are being ordered from CAF and Swiss train-builder Stadler.

CAF has been named by KeolisAmey as the preferred bidder to supply and maintain 44 two-car and 26 three-car units for rural and suburban routes across Wales by September 2022 with a further seven two-car sets to be delivered by September 2024. The announcement came after KeolisAmey was awarded the contract by the Welsh Government to run the 15-year Wales and Borders rail franchise from October 2018.

Colin Lea, mobilisation director at KeolisAmey Wales Cymru, said: "These new trains will set a new standard of travel comfort and accessibility for the next decade, they will be made for Wales and by Wales, as they will be assembled in a new CAF factory in Newport, creating hundreds of new jobs.

"We would like to thank CAF for working collaboratively with us to design trains, which, in line with KeolisAmey values, put the passenger needs at their heart, with state-of-the-art passenger features, ample legroom and seats aligned with windows to enjoy the wonderful scenery of the routes they will serve."

Welsh Government Economy Secretary, Ken Skates, added: "Our £5bn investment in the new rail services will deliver not only vastly improved train services, but also real job opportunities and economic benefits that will be felt in communities right across Wales."

The high-performance DMUs will be built at CAF's new facility at the Celtic Business Park site in Newport, which

Services between Cardiff Bay, Treherbert, Merthyr Tydfil and Aberdare via Pontypridd are to be transformed into a high-frequency tram-train operation using Stadler 'CityLink' hybrid electric/battery vehicles. TRANSPORT FOR WALES

porterbrook

is scheduled for completion in autumn 2018. They are based on the 'Civity UK' platform, designed for commuter and regional services, featuring the latest safety technology combined with exacting interior design specifications for customer comfort, including air-conditioning and wi-fi.

METRO OPERATION

In addition, Stadler will supply 11 four-car 'FLIRT' DEMUs for the South Wales Metro, seven three-car and 17 four-car tri-mode (electric, battery and diesel) 'FLIRTs' for the Barry/Penarth-Cardiff-Rhymney route and 36 three-car Stadler CityLink tram-trains to link the Treherbert, Aberdare and Merthyr Tydfil lines with a new on-street tram route through the Cardiff Bay area.

Deliveries of the CAF DMUs will start in the second half of 2021, with the first Metro vehicles due at the end of that year, 'FLIRT' DEMUs in mid-2022 and tri-mode 'FLIRTs' in mid-2023.

The use of tri-mode trains fitted with batteries and diesel engines will enable electric trains to be introduced without the need for expensive modifications to structures such as bridges and tunnels. Discontinuous electrification planned for the South Wales valleys will avoid disruptive civil engineering work at 55 locations.

In central Cardiff, the Queen Street-Cardiff branch will be extended via on-street running to The Flourish, one of four new stations in the city. The others will be Loudoun Square, Crwys Road and Gabalfa.

Total capacity across Wales will increase by 65%, including 45% more seats into Cardiff and 294 extra Sunday services that will increase the operator's mileage by 22% from 2019. Overall, 95% of rail journeys in Wales will be made on new trains by 2024 and the average age of the fleet will fall from 25 years today to just seven years by 2023.

Highlights of the new service will include a doubling of frequencies on the Metro routes, with four trains per hour on the Treherbert, Merthyr and Aberdare lines from 2022 and Rhymney from 2023, plus two trains per hour on Sundays. The Ebbw Vale line service will be doubled from 2021, with the Vale of Glamorgan line following suit from 2023.

CASCADES

Before that, much of the current fleet will be replaced by trains cascaded from other parts of the network. During 2019, five Class 769 'Flex' bi-mode trains (converted from Class 319s), five ex-GWR Class 153s and 12 Class 170 DMUs (eight three-car, four

> For the Rhymney-Cardiff-Penarth/Barry route, TfW is ordering tri-mode (diesel/electric/battery) 'FLIRTs' from Stadler in Switzerland, providing a significant increase in quality over the current fleet. Diesel-electric 'FLIRTs' will also be built for the Cardiff-Maesteg, Bridgend and Ebbw Vale routes. TRANSPORT FOR WALES

two-car sets released by Greater Anglia) will join the Wales & Borders fleet as an interim measure. For the thrice-daily Cardiff-Holyhead service, three shortened and refurbished sets of Mk 4 stock (four passenger coaches plus DVT) released by LNER will replace the current Mk 3 sets in December 2019.

TfW has also ordered five three-car Class 230 diesel/battery hybrid trains from Vivarail to replace Class 150s on the Wrexham-Chester/Bidston routes. The fleet is due to move to Wales for final testing and commissioning in early 2019. The extensively rebuilt ex-London Underground 'D78' trains will be the first to come into service under the new franchise.

Adrian Shooter, CEO of Vivarail, said: "This is a very exciting day for us and we are proud to be supplying the first of the new trains for Wales. With this hybrid fleet we will deliver a train that is clean, green and reliable, making use

> CAF is to build 77 'Civity UK' diesel trains for the new Wales & Borders operation between 2021 and 2024. The DMUs will be assembled at its new factory near Newport as part of a commitment to build up to 50% of the replacement train fleet in Wales. TRANSPORT FOR WALES

Above left: An artist's impression of the CAF 'Civity UK' DMU for long-distance and rural lines in Wales. Similar trains are being built for West Midlands Railway. TRANSPORT FOR WALES

Above right: A new on-street tramway is planned between the current Cardiff Bay (formerly Bute Road) terminus and The Flourish in the redeveloped Cardiff Bay area. TRANSPORT FOR WALES

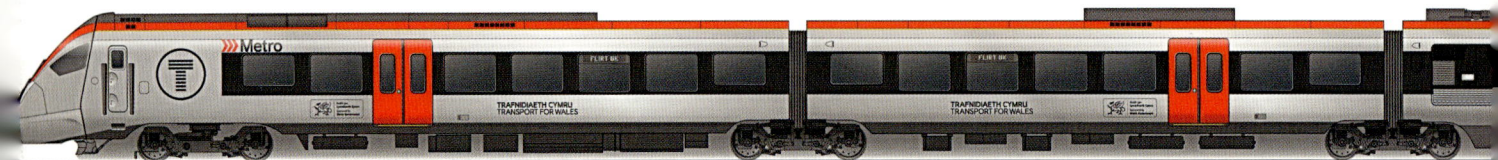

porterbrook

A broadside impression of the planned three-car CAF DMUs. TRANSPORT FOR WALES

of GPS systems to cut out the diesel engines in stations and environmentally-sensitive areas.

"Our trains will come into service in summer 2019 and will form the flagship fleet for Wales and Borders."

As well as wide and spacious interiors, the trains will have a universal access toilet, wi-fi, air-conditioning, USB charging ports and plug sockets. There will be a range of seating layouts and space for bikes and luggage.

The design and build of the three-car trains is already underway at Vivarail's two sites and orders have been placed with the leading supplier of universal access toilets based in Cwmbran.

The fleet of five trains will move to Wales for final testing and commissioning in early 2019.

£1.9BN INVESTMENT

The fleet changes will mean that Class 142/143 'Pacers' and Mk 3 stock will be eliminated by the end of 2019, with the Class 153s, 158s and Class 175s – and the yet-to-be-seen Class 769s – all going during 2022. The Class 150/2 fleet, which is currently being refurbished to meet new PRM-TSI accessibility rules, is expected to continue until the end of 2023.

KeolisAmey has been awarded a 15-year contract to operate Wales & Borders services and to act as a development partner for the South Wales/Central

Metro network. It will replace Arriva Trains Wales on October 14. In return, it is to invest £800m in new trains, £194m on improving all 247 stations in Wales and £738m in the South Wales Metro – a total of £1.9bn. In September 2019, Network Rail will transfer ownership of the future 'Central Metro' infrastructure to TfW as a precursor to the redevelopment of the network. Investments by the Welsh Government and other stakeholders will take spending to £5bn over the 15-year deal.

Transport for Wales (TfW) is a not-for-profit company wholly owned by the Welsh Government, intended to provide technical advice to the Government and deliver its transport policies.

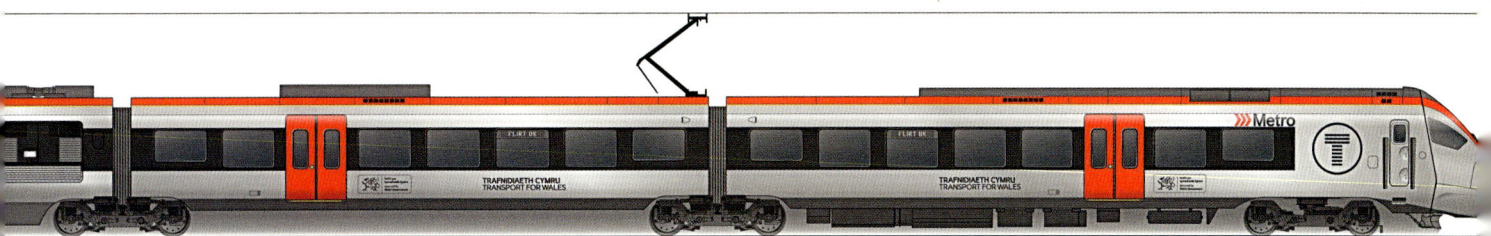

EXTENDING ASSET LIFE

While new train fleets make the headlines, the owners of existing trains are keen to see their expensive assets continue to 'earn their keep' and with a glut of spare trains on the horizon they are having to become increasingly innovative to attract new business.

porterbrook

On June 19, 2018, the driving cars from Northern EMUs Nos. 319434 and 319456 near the completion of their conversion into Class 769 bi-mode trains with diesel power packs at the former Brush works in Loughborough, now owned by Wabtec Faiveley UK. Northern has eight Class 769 'Flex' trains on order from Porterbrook. BEN JONES

Production

Production Engineering

porterbrook

FLEX:

The 'go anywhere' train

With so many new trains being delivered and electrification schemes shelved, Porterbrook and Brush Traction are using their engineering expertise to convert surplus Thameslink commuter trains into 'go anywhere' bi-mode trains.

When you've invested millions of pounds in maintaining and updating trains to bring them up to modern standards, what do you do when those trains become surplus to requirements soon afterwards?

That was the problem facing Derby-based train leasing company Porterbrook a few years ago, as several large fleets of electric trains were rendered redundant by massive new train orders.

In the case of Thameslink, 86 four-car Class 319 dual-voltage EMUs built between 1987 and 1990 have been replaced by new Siemens Class 700s over the last three years. Most have recently been refurbished and fitted with controlled emission toilets, passenger information systems and PRM-TSI-compliant accessible toilets to keep them in service beyond December 2019. Originally, much of the fleet was expected to switch to GWR's Thames Valley commuter operation, with others moving to Northern. The curtailment of Great Western main line electrification and GWR's decision to purchase new Class 387 EMUs for the remaining electric services left more than 60 '319s' without work beyond 2018.

The project started as far back as 2014 when, inspired by the Bombardier/Network Rail Independently Powered Electric Multiple Unit (IPEMU) experiment (which saw batteries fitted to a Class 379 EMU), Porterbrook challenged its engineering team to

Wabtec Faiveley in Loughborough was chosen by Porterbrook as its development partner for the 'Flex' project. On June 19, 2018, the driving trailers from Nos. 319434 and 319456 await the installation of their diesel power packs prior to the start of dynamic testing. BEN JONES

porterbrook

create their own IPEMU concept using Class 319s.

At that time, the Government was still committed to a rolling programme of electrification, but many routes were still unlikely to be wired, even in the longer term. Only 42% of the British rail network is electrified, compared to anywhere between 50% and virtually 100% in mainland Europe. Spotting an opportunity for a flexible train that could take advantage of the gradually increasing electrified network and operate under its own power elsewhere, Porterbrook started to investigate the options for trains that could easily, and reliably, switch between an external power supply and an on-board energy source. Helen

the risks with us by helping to fund the design work."

In common with other ex-BR Mk3-based EMUs, the Class 319s have one powered intermediate vehicle and three trailers, with the underbody area of the two driving cars relatively uncluttered. The new bi-mode concept centred around installing a diesel power pack and an alternator under each Driving Trailer Second (DTS) vehicle.

Helen continues: "We had to check if they would take the extra weight, but we knew that a Class 150 DMU driving car [of similar design] was heavier."

Simon Evans, group innovations director at Wabtec Faiveley UK, which owns the Brush Traction works in Loughborough, was

companies [TOCs] that the concept was sound. The timetable analysis proved to be very useful for us."

The new engine rafts feature a power pack with an MAN D2876 390kW diesel engine and an ABB alternator. The design of the raft is similar to that used on Bombardier 'Turbostar' DMUs and it is designed to be removed or installed quickly with the assistance of a special lifting platform.

Simon explains: "The MAN engines have a rail pedigree and are compliant with Stage IIIb emissions rules. Their maximum rating is 390kW, but we decided to have them working at less than that to give ourselves some 'headroom'.

"In service, the two engines will deliver around 720kW at the DC link (just under 1000hp), which is somewhat less than the 1.2MW available in electric mode, but in general speeds are expected to be lower when working on diesel and this arrangement gives good power in the mid-range. Performance should be comparable to a Class 150."

For comparison, each Class 150 vehicle has a 213kW (285hp) Cummins diesel engine, delivering 570hp for a standard two-car set.

Simon continues: "A '319' body is almost identical to a Class 150, so we knew the diesel components and exhaust systems would fit, although the positioning of some of the existing electrical equipment resulted in some convoluted exhaust runs."

Other modifications include new electronics cubicles and two Ethernet communications buses running the length of each train.

Helen explains: "The two engines have to 'talk' to each other, so we added two Ethernet connections, one for wi-fi and PIS and one for traction. The existing train control wiring has also been retained. It's essential that the two power packs work together and don't fight

> ## "Rebuilding can often be more difficult than building from new. Making the existing and new components work together can be a real challenge."
> **Helen Simpson, innovation & development manager, Porterbrook**

Simpson, innovation and development manager for Porterbrook, was there at the beginning.

She says: "We looked at diesel engines, batteries, supercapacitors [electrical storage devices capable of providing a short-term boost of energy], hydrogen and flywheels, but only diesel offered the high energy density, good range and proven capabilities we were looking for.

"We selected Brush Traction in Loughborough as our development partner. Porterbrook funded the feasibility study, while Brush shared

also there from the start of the project.

"For us it was, and is, an investment in the future. We think it has 'legs'. Not only does it present opportunities for similar modifications of other fleets, it is also creating an engineering base for other projects, and developing engineering expertise in the UK."

Appropriately, given the flexibility the new train could offer, it was soon branded 'Flex' by the team.

COMPUTER MODEL

"We had to run numerous computer models for 'Flex' to see if it would perform as required with a passenger load on the various routes and schedules it might be asked to work," says Helen.

"This assured the train operating

porterbrook

FLEX
by porterbrook

each other, so Wabtec had to design a sophisticated new electronics package to oversee the traction supply and trick the existing electrics into thinking they are working on their usual DC supply."

However, to keep things as simple as possible in the driving cabs, extra equipment is limited to new fire warning and engine stop buttons. This should make conversion courses relatively straightforward for drivers already passed on Class 319s.

Once passed for service, the bi-mode Class 769s will still be able to work in multiple with their dual-voltage Class 319 sisters. Helen and Simon also say that the '769s' should be generally quieter than Class 15x 'Sprinters' because the power pack is largely enclosed and separated from the floorpan by two sets of substantial rubber mountings that will absorb vibration.

CHALLENGES

It's widely known now that the project is running some months late. The first Arriva Rail North Class 769s should have entered passenger service in May 2018, but as this publication went to press, the first set was being prepared for initial dynamic testing at the Great Central Railway, close to the Brush factory in Loughborough.

What challenges did the team face in converting these trains into bi-modes?

"Rebuilding can often be more difficult than building from new," admits Helen. "Making the existing and new components work together can be a real challenge."

Simon interjects: "Our biggest engineering challenge of the whole project was the new electronic control cubicle, which controls local power on the driving cars. All the new integration control electronics and electric systems were designed in-house by Brush – we don't buy them in and bolt them on.

"Nearly all that kind of engineering knowledge has disappeared from the UK, but projects like this are vital for retaining knowledge and skills. It also ensures that we get exactly what we want, and not what someone else thinks we need."

He adds: "For this project we had three stakeholders – Porterbrook, Arriva Rail North and the Department for Transport (DfT) – which could have been problematic. However, we have had very clear communications across all departments, from operations to engineering, and all have been involved to inform the design process and changes throughout. For example, the maintenance team suggested a change to the filling arrangement of the AdBlue [a fuel additive that reduces harmful emissions from diesel engines] filler to ensure it is the same as the new

CAF Class 195 DMUs at depots. There will always be compromises, but the key is to find a balance that keeps as many people happy as possible."

Helen continues: "We have had to fit a track circuit actuator [TCA], which turned out to be much more complex than anticipated, and a fire barrier, but otherwise there haven't been too many unexpected horrors!

"For a build of their era, the Class 319 fleet is remarkably standard, but there are minor technical differences between the '319/3' and

> "Our biggest engineering challenge was the new electronic control cubicle, which controls local power on the driving cars. All the new electronics and electrics were designed in-house by Brush – we don't buy them in and bolt them on."
> **Simon Evans, group innovations director, Wabtec Faiveley UK**

'319/4' and the four sub-fleets created since.

"Weight management has also been an issue, although removing the third-rail shoegear from the Northern and W&B sets will save 300-400kg. However, the GWR sets (see next page) will be retaining their DC capability, and will gain air-cooling equipment, so their weight will be more difficult to keep in check."

In total, more than 60 engineers have spent more than 60,000 hours on more than 2500 drawings developing more than 3500 components for the 'Flex' conversions.

porterbrook

Top right: Looking more like Class 150 vehicles after the installation of exhaust stacks on their inner ends for the new diesel power packs, Nos. 77356 and 77448 are prepared for their new roles at Loughborough on June 19. BEN JONES

Bottom right: The first production 'Flex' power pack containing the MAN diesel engine and ABB alternator. BEN JONES

The pre-production engine rafts have spent hundreds of hours on a specially constructed test rig at Loughborough and every production raft will be 'shaken down' on the same rig before it is installed on a train. The tests take the engines through a full cycle, including taking them beyond their notional maximum output to ensure they have the capacity to deal with power surges.

However, in service the engines will ramp up to a steady speed, run at a fixed rate and supply electric current for the traction motors via the alternator. As diesel engines are 'happier' when running at a constant rate, this should ensure better reliability, longer engine life and greater efficiency than the constant powering up and down experienced by standard DMU engines.

GROWING INTEREST

An initial order for eight 'Flex' sets from Arriva Rail North in December 2016 was followed by five for Arriva Trains Wales in July 2017 (Wales & Borders from October 2018), an order that has an option for a further four sets. Once development and testing is complete, the whole conversion process – and the engine raft assembly in particular – is designed to be easy to 'productionise'. This should mean that Northern and Wales & Borders receive their sets during 2019, adding extra capacity and, in the case of W&B, releasing Class 150/2s for PRM-TSI modifications.

Next to opt for 'Flex' was Great Western Railway, which placed an order for 19 tri-mode (25kv AC, 750v DC third-rail and diesel) trains for Thames Valley local services and the Reading-Gatwick route in early-2018. These trains will have a higher specification than their sisters, and will feature air-cooling equipment and upgraded interiors, as well as the unique ability to operate on non-electrified lines, 25kv AC overhead on the Great Western Main Line and the Southern

Region third-rail network. The first set is expected to appear in 2019, replacing Class 165/166 DMUs and freeing GWR Class 387s for their new role with Heathrow Express. Knorr-Bremse at Wolverton has been contracted to refurbish the trains.

Will the trains deliver what operators require of them?

Helen says: "Our target for diesel operation was a 500-mile range, but we expect them now to manage 700-800 miles, which should mean they can run for two or three days before they need refuelling. "Obviously, the more they work on 25kv AC electric supply, the longer that period will be."

After testing at the Great Central Railway in August, the first 'Flex' set will venture out onto the main line for further dynamic testing at higher speeds as part of the approvals process. Currently, it is hoped that the first trains will enter passenger service with Northern on the Manchester Airport-Windermere route in December.

DEVELOPING THE CONCEPT

Looking further ahead, Porterbrook is keen to develop the 'Flex' concept and create more bi-mode trains for a variety of uses. With modern DMUs continuing to be in high demand, the leasing company is hopeful that it will be able to find new homes for much of the Class 319 fleet – many of which are now in storage.

Porterbrook is keen to emphasise that 'Flex' is not limited to passenger duties, and it is working with partners in the intermodal freight business to

develop ideas for lightweight, high-speed freight and parcel trains. Taking advantage of their go-anywhere, bi-mode capability, converted Class 319s with internal racking could be a useful tool for freight companies wanting to tap into the increasingly important high-value overnight parcel business.

The leasing company is also working with the UK Rail Research and Innovation Network (UKRRIN) to develop ideas for 'convertible' vehicles fitted with seats designed to concertina, creating space for parcels, luggage and cycles, as demand dictates.

Looking beyond the '319s', Porterbrook is also examining possibilities for the South Western Railway Class 455 EMU fleet, which will be replaced by 2021. The modernised SWR '455s', which received Vossloh-Kiepe AC traction packages in 2016-17, are likely to find new homes elsewhere on the third-rail network, but are viewed as good candidates for conversion to self-powered or bi-mode operation.

Interestingly, Porterbrook is also hinting at the possible conversion of some Southern Class 377 EMUs into bi-mode trains to replace Class 171 DMUs on the London-Uckfield and Ashford-Hastings routes.

This fascinating story will develop over the coming years and it is good to see a leasing company prepared to invest in British engineering and innovative home-grown technologies to prolong the lives of trains that might otherwise be heading for the scrapyard.

Thanks to Porterbrook and Wabtec Faiveley UK for their assistance with this article.

Locomotive refurbishment

One of the most surprising developments of recent years is the return of many ex-BR diesel locomotives to the main line, providing a cheaper and more flexible solution for lighter duties and short-term requirements.

One of the most obvious trends of the last couple of years is the remarkable revival of many older diesel locomotives. From 60-year-old English Electric Class 20s delivering new Underground trains to utterly transformed Class 73s hauling Scottish sleepers, dozens of machines have been liberated from scrapyards and preserved railways to take up a second (or even third) career on the main line. Commercial railway companies must have a clear economic and operational case for taking this route – these machines have to earn their keep in the modern world.

Since the early years of privatisation in the late-1990s, preserved or privately-owned diesels have sporadically returned to the main line for railtour or short-term 'spot hire' work, but the recent renaissance of ex-BR motive power is a response to various factors affecting contemporary freight and infrastructure operators.

Direct Rail Services (DRS) set the precedent for reviving older diesels in 1995-98 when it acquired 15 Class 20s and had them extensively modernised by Brush (Nos. 20301-305) and Wabtec Doncaster (Nos. 20306-315) for hauling nuclear flask trains. In the absence of any new type of low/medium power diesel locomotive, the '20s' offered a quick and proven solution to the new operator's go-anywhere requirements.

A shortage of new locomotive designs to the UK loading gauge remains an issue today, especially now that Class 66 production has ceased. Stadler's 3750hp Class 68 is the only straight diesel locomotive currently on offer to UK operators, and with a Route Availability rating of seven (RA7) it is barred from large parts of the network – especially at its extremities.

Add in the high leasing costs of complex, powerful machines costing around £3-4 million each, long lead times for new orders and strict emissions rules for diesel engines and existing machines with 'grandfather rights' for operation on the network start to look more attractive.

A similar situation exists across mainland Europe, where sales of large diesel locomotives have been depressed for more than a decade. Although the 'big three' train builders – Bombardier, Siemens and Alstom – all offer diesel versions of their main locomotive 'platforms' (TRAXX, Vectron and Prima respectively), sales are far outweighed by their electric equivalents.

With a limited pool of customers and comparatively low sales potential in the UK, there's little incentive for the big rail groups to invest in designing bespoke locomotives for British operators. The great success of the EMD Class 66 lay not just in the fact that it was reasonably cheap, reliable and could be delivered fairly quickly, but also because there was nothing else on offer.

Operators looking for modern small or medium power diesels in Europe can call on alternative suppliers such as Vossloh Locomotives in Kiel and CZ Loko of the Czech Republic, but to date these have shown no obvious interest in the UK market. A version of the Vossloh DE18 – a single-cab diesel-electric available in the 1100 to 1800kW power range (1475hp to 2400hp) – built to the British loading gauge, could be an extremely useful tool to replace ex-BR Type 1 to 3 diesels, but we may have to wait some time for such a machine to come along.

Many older locomotives have been reactivated or refurbished for hauling new trains around the network. Hired by Rail Operations Group from Europhoenix, No. 37601 *Perseus* hauls new Crossrail 'Aventra' No. 345021 past Chellaston, near Derby, working from Barton-under-Needwood to Old Dalby on January 17, 2018.
STEVE DONALD

porterbrook

In the meantime, several rail engineering companies have carved themselves a lucrative niche by offering thoroughly overhauled and modernised locomotives built between the late-1950s and late-1970s.

VARIED WORKLOAD

In many cases ex-BR traction has been called back to the front line to provide extra short-term capacity during traffic peaks, or to free more modern and powerful locomotives from lightweight or short distance workings where they are not being used to their full potential.

This work includes Network Rail test and infrastructure management (IM) trains, rolling stock moves and new train deliveries, on-track plant transfers and short-term or one-off freight contracts.

GB Railfreight has been a prime example of this, hiring Class 20s to deliver new Underground trains from Derby to London and using ex-Riviera Trains Class 47/8s on local sand trips around Doncaster. In both cases, older machines provided an ideal, cost-effective solution and freed Class 66s for more mainstream intermodal

or bulk freight work. The recent acquisition of 16 3300hp Class 56s from UK Rail Leasing is another response to the current shortage of available modern locomotives for heavy freight work.

In contrast, DRS has employed its fleet of modernised ex-BR diesels on a wide range of work, from lightweight nuclear trains to heavy Anglo-Scottish intermodals on the West Coast Main Line. The DRS fleet has constantly evolved since the late-1990s, drawing in second-hand Class 20s, 33s, 37s, 47s and 57s, but also introducing modern Class 66s and 68s, and Class 88 electro-diesels, on the most demanding duties.

Since 2015, it has also had to return a number of electric train supply (ETS) fitted Class 37/4s to passenger work with

Northern and Greater Anglia due to DMU shortages. DRS has invested hundreds of thousands of pounds per locomotive in heavy overhauls and modernisation for its Class 37/4s, some of which were stored in the open air for many years after withdrawal.

These locomotives were prepared for their return to traffic by LORAM (formerly Rail Vehicle

DRS was the first operator after privatisation to buy withdrawn diesels and invest in complete re-engineering to give them a second main line career. On March 8, a line of stored Class 20/3s await a decision on their future at Barrow Hill. BEN JONES

One of the most astonishing revivals of recent years is the rebuilding of redundant Class 73s with new 1600hp MTU diesel engines, transforming them into 'go anywhere' machines. On July 26, 2017, GB Railfreight's No. 73964 *Jeanette* and No. 73965 pass Barrow upon Soar on the Midland Main Line near Loughborough with the 13.30 West Hampstead Thameslink-Derby RTC Network Rail test train. PAUL BIGGS

general' overhaul on, for example, a Class 37, can cost in the region of £750,000, so while it's not a cheap option, it costs significantly less than buying new, and it brings added advantage of using proven, reliable (if outdated) equipment.

MODERN EQUIPMENT

While much of the cost centres around overhauling ageing power units and repairing years of neglect and corrosion to bodywork, there also has to be a significant investment in up-to-date signalling, safety and monitoring equipment. For locomotives that have, in some cases, been off the network since the late-1990s, modernisation work includes the installation of Train Protection & Warning System (TPWS), On-Train Monitoring & Recording (OTMR), Driver Safety Device (DSD) and GSM-R telephone equipment costing tens of thousands of pounds, plus modern headlights and new high-impact windscreens with toughened safety glass and reinforced frames.

According to Andy, overhaul costs can vary depending on the scope of the re-engineering and customer requirements. In the case of the two 'Ultra' Class 73s re-engineered by RVEL/LORAM in 2014/15 to replace Class 31s on Network Rail's ultrasonic test trains, the donor locomotives were stripped

Engineering Ltd), which is a major player in the specialist refurbishment and overhaul of older rail vehicles. In recent years it has expanded its operation at the former BR Railway Technical Centre in Derby to cope with demand from customers including Network Rail, First Great Western, DRS and Colas Railfreight.

LORAM UK commercial director Andy Houghton explains why operators have recently turned to his company to help meet their traction requirements: "It is a cost-effective method of creating reliable, fuel and maintenance efficient locomotives. Operators can gain the advantages of modern equipment without the huge costs involved with the introduction of a new locomotive."

Other industry sources suggest that a full 'heavy

Below left: Two Class 73s rebuilt by RVEL (now LORAM) for Network Rail were taken back to bare metal bodyshells and transformed into modern electro-diesels with two Cummins 750hp engines, new traction equipment and modernised cabs. BEN JONES

Below right: More than 60 years since their introduction, a small number of English Electric-built Class 20s continue to earn a living on the main line network. GB Railfreight No. 20901 rests between duties at Barrow Hill on March 8, 2017. BEN JONES

porterbrook

back to bare metal bodyshells and rebuilt from the ground up.

"You need to consider the new control systems that are required with the new engines, traction systems, driver controls, brake systems, and even such things as air-conditioning," he elaborates.

The rebuilding of the 'Ultra 73s' went much further than most projects, replacing the original 600hp English Electric power unit and with two 750hp Cummins QSK19 engines (as used on Voyager DEMUs) and sophisticated modern electronics to create a 1500hp 'gen-set' unit capable of working anywhere on the British network.

Andy says: "Class 73 was chosen due to its 'go-anywhere' capabilities. It has good route availability. There was also a number of spare locomotives available for re-engineering at the time we were looking at it. However, the 'Ultra' gen-set technology can be applied to almost all existing locomotive platforms."

Redundant and preserved Class 73s also provided the basis for another remarkable re-engineering project that has taken the electro-diesels far beyond their original Southern Region home. In 2014-16, Brush Loughborough rebuilt 11 locomotives for GB Railfreight, including two of the prototype 'JA' batch (Nos. 73005/006) dating from 1962. Again, the original EE power unit was replaced, in this case with a 1600hp MTU4000 engine and modern control electronics. Nos. 73961-965 retain their 750v DC third-rail capability and are used for Network Rail engineering trains on the Southern Region and beyond, while Nos. 73966-971 are allocated to Caledonian Sleeper services, working from Edinburgh to Aberdeen, Fort William and Inverness. While they have suffered from teething troubles, including alternator problems, they provide a capable, if unconventional, solution to powering the diesel legs of the CS operation.

TRUSTY TYPE 3S

Although withdrawals started in the late-1980s, the privatised railway has so far proved unable to manage without that most versatile of mixed traffic diesels – the English Electric Class 37s. DRS has, of course, been the most high-profile user over the last 15 years, but ex-EWS machines continue to reappear in new guises, along with former DRS machines managing a third (or even a fourth) lease of life with new operators.

Several former 'wrecks' and preserved Class 37s have recently returned to the main line with Colas, powering NR test trains all over the country.

Having started by hiring in traction from other companies, Rail Operations Group (ROG) now has its own fleet of ex-BR locomotives too – buying five Class 47/8s from Riviera Trains (Nos. 47812/815/843/847/848), hiring Nos. 37800/884 from Europhoenix and acquiring No. 37608 from DRS in 2016.

The two 'heavyweight' Class 37/7s were restored to main line condition by Harry Needle Railroad Co. (HNRC) at Barrow Hill (No. 37884) and UK Rail Leasing (No. 37800).

HNRC has been active in the UK locomotive engineering and hire market for more than two decades, and has become a market leader, competing with multi-national giants such as Wabtec and LORAM, despite having just 32 staff. HNRC supplies overhauled industrial shunters and ex-BR Class 08s, 20s, 37s and 47s for a variety of customers, including DRS, Colas and Network Rail.

As someone whose core business is built around restoring these older machines, why does Harry think more and more are making a comeback?

"Rebuilding a Class 37 or a Class 47 will cost you around £600,000, but that will put it back on the main line for 10 years, whereas a new Class 68 could cost you £4m. It's more cost-effective

and it gives you a proven, reliable machine that is compliant with the modern railway.

"We can also offer a 'power upgrade' if the customer wants it – for example we can replace the English Electric power unit in a Class 37 with an MTU4000 engine, similar to those now used in HST power cars. De-rating it to 1750hp will prolong the engine's life too."

Harry continues: "I think these locos have got at least another 15 years left in them. It's not cost-effective to build new RA5 locos to our bespoke loading gauge."

The award for greatest survivors though must go to the Class 20s, which celebrate their 60th anniversary this year. HNRC owns 22 of the class, eight of which are passed for the main line and used by GBRf, and it also hires others to industrial users such as Lafarge and Tata/British Steel. Robust, reliable, cheap to run and able to go almost anywhere, the '20s' continue to prove their worth, especially when working as a 2000hp pair.

Another company seeking to provide solutions for operators requiring diesel locomotives is UK Rail Leasing, based at the former Leicester TMD. It also provides maintenance, overhaul and 'spot hire' services and customers have included ROG, Freightliner and Devon & Cornwall Railways (DCR).

After EWS took delivery of 250 Class 66s in 1998-2000, and other freight companies followed suit, the subsequent cull of older diesels led most of us to believe that we'd only see these locomotives from the 1960s and 1970s in action on preserved railways as the 21st century bedded in. Although they're fewer in number than they once were, these survivors are proving that there's plenty of life in the 'old dogs' yet – and that, with dedicated engineering support from the likes of HNRC, Brush and LORAM, they will still be playing an important role on modern railways well into the 2020s.

Older locos can provide a cost-effective solution for shunting major yards, short trip workings and lightweight stock transfers, freeing powerful and modern machines for more lucrative work. On November 11, 2016, Freightliner's No. 47830 *Beeching's Legacy* sits outside the company's new depot at Crewe Basford Hall. BEN JONES

porterbrook

Welcome back 'Wessex Electrics'

One of the most surprising developments of recent years was FirstGroup/MTR's decision to revive and modernise 18 stored Class 442 EMUs for the Waterloo-Portsmouth route.

37 884

porterbrook

Heading for storage at Eastleigh Works, a Class 442 set, released by Southern, is towed along the former London & South Western Main Line at Pot Bridge near Winchfield on August 12, 2016 by Rail Operations Group diesel No. 37884. Class 442s could return to this route with Grand Southern Railway if the open access operator is given permission to start running trains on the Southampton-London route.
CHRISTOPHER WILSON

SWR Class 442

Operator:	South Western Railway
Built:	1988-89 (rebuilt 2018-19)
Introduced:	Late-2018
No. ordered:	18
No. of cars per train:	Five
Numbers:	TBC
Order value:	£45m
Routes:	Waterloo-Portsmouth Harbour
Power supply:	750v DC third-rail
Max speed:	100mph
Power rating:	1.2MW
Formation:	DTSO(A)+TSO+ MBC+TSO(W)+ DTSO(B)
Capacity:	TBC
Features:	Air-conditioning, new AC traction package, inter-city interiors
Owner/finance:	Angel Trains

South Western Railway (SWR) has awarded Kiepe Electric UK a contract to undertake a £45 million refurbishment of 18 ex-BR Class 442 electric trains for use on fast London Waterloo-Portsmouth services from December 2018.

These popular inter-city trains were introduced in 1988-89 by BR's Network SouthEast (NSE) sector and worked the Waterloo-Southampton-Bournemouth-Weymouth corridor for many years. Procured to coincide with the extension of third-rail electrification beyond Bournemouth in 1988, they replaced late-1960s vintage '4-REP' and '4-TC' combinations, the latter of which were powered by Class 33/1 diesels west of Bournemouth.

Reusing traction equipment recovered from the 'REPs', 24 five-car sets were built at Derby Litchurch Lane works (now Bombardier's UK plant) and based at Bournemouth depot.

Class 442 is based on the BR Mk3 bodyshell design, but has a number of features distinguishing it from conventional slam-door Mk3s. Their vehicle length is 23m and all vehicles are air-conditioned and have power-operated plug doors for passengers. When new, they suffered a number of technical issues that affected their reliability, but they went on to become one of the most reliable fleets on the network.

After privatisation they were sold to Angel Trains and leased by South West Trains until 2007. After a period in store, they were leased to Southern for Gatwick Express services from London Victoria to Gatwick Airport and Brighton. Although they were not well suited to airport work, they remained with Southern/Gatwick Express until they were replaced by new 'Electrostars' in 2016.

Amazingly, a second reprieve was announced in March 2017 when FirstGroup/MTR wrestled the South Western franchise away from Stagecoach after 21 years.

As well as 750 new 'Aventra' EMU vehicles, SWR announced that it would reintroduce 18 of the 24 trains to improve its fast Waterloo-Portsmouth Harbour services via Guildford, Haslemere and Petersfield. Currently, SWR uses Siemens Class 450 EMUs designed for semi-fast and outer-suburban work, which aren't suitable for this key main line route.

Modernisation work is being undertaken by Kiepe at Eastleigh Works and is intended to increase the reliability and efficiency of the units. This includes the replacement of life-expired English Electric DC traction equipment with an AC package incorporating IGBT technology from Kiepe Electric Düsseldorf.

New brake controls from Knorr-Bremse Rail Vehicle Systems will add regenerative braking capability, improving the environmental performance and efficiency of the trains and lowering operating costs.

New seats and Axminster carpets will be installed, along with real-time passenger information, LED lighting and passenger wi-fi. There will be at-seat charging sockets in First and Standard classes, and table-top inductive charging facilities in First Class. There will be spaces for passengers with reduced mobility and accessible toilets for the first time, making the SWR '442s' compliant with new PRM-TSI accessibility rules. Angel Trains, which still owns the fleet, will fund the refurbishment and recover the investment through higher leasing charges.

Neil Drury, SWR engineering director, said: "We are delighted to have appointed Kiepe Electric to carry out the refurbishment and retraction of our incoming fleet of Class 442 trains.

"They have an excellent track record in this field and we know that they will produce a high-quality product for our customers that will include refurbished interiors, new information systems and improved performance."

By the summer of 2018, the first sets had been completed and moved back to their spiritual home at Bournemouth depot to commence training and approvals work. However, main line testing had not commenced by the time this publication went to print. The 18 trains will receive a variant of SWR's new grey/silver livery and will be based at Bournemouth. SWR expects to have the first '442s' back in passenger service from December 2018, although this will depend on their gaining approval from Network Rail and SWR for use in their modified form.

AND THEN THERE WERE SIX...

SWR's decision to take 18 units leaves six available for other operators. In November 2016, Arriva's open access subsidiary Alliance Rail announced plans to use Class 442s on a new inter-city service between Waterloo and Southampton Central. Alliance Rail planned a full internal refurbishment of the sets, but did not expect to undertake the same traction upgrade as SWR. Seven weekday return paths were identified and offered to Alliance by NR as part of the 2018 timetable planning process, but unfortunately the Office of Rail and Road (ORR) declined to authorise GSR's proposals in August 2018. Although it is recognised that there are overcrowding problems on this route, the ORR concluded that GSR did not have enough suitable rolling stock and the service would not generate sufficient new income. NR and SWR were also concerned that GSR services could have a detrimental impact on overall train performance on the route.

Stored Class 442 sets await new homes at Potter Group's Ely sidings on November 25, 2016. PETER FOSTER

porterbrook

Life begins at 40
for revamped ScotRail and GWR HSTs

Released from their traditional duties by new Intercity Express Trains, many InterCity 125 vehicles have been snapped up to improve services in Scotland and the West Country.

New and refurbished trains, a revitalised InterCity network, a rolling programme of electrification and numerous other improvements are part of the ScotRail Alliance's ambitious plan to increase passenger numbers and satisfaction on what is already one of the country's best performing large operators.

However, one of the most high-profile franchise commitments for Abellio ScotRail is the introduction of extensively refurbished ex-GWR HST sets on internal inter-city services. What difference will they make to Scottish passengers?

Clearly enthused by the prospect, ScotRail Alliance managing director Alex Hynes says: "I think they're going to be amazing. I think the HSTs will be a game-changer for us.

"We know our customers already use them in preference to our DMUs [on the Inverness and Aberdeen routes served by VTEC] and our short sets are going to go like the wind.

"The power cars have been refurbished several times already, but the coaches will gain new sliding doors, controlled emission toilets and the interiors will be 'tartaned up'. We're keeping the very nice GWR leather seats in First Class, but Standard Class will get better seats that line up with the windows, more tables and better seat pitch.

"Tourism is a big market for us – we've got some of the most beautiful railway journeys in the world and people want to see that scenery."

He adds: "We're bringing back the InterCity brand too – the HSTs will be branded InterCity ScotRail. We had to get permission from the DfT, as it still owns the rights."

ScotRail's 26 short-formation HST sets will deliver a significant increase in quality on inter-city services between Scotland's seven cities (Edinburgh, Glasgow, Dundee, Aberdeen, Inverness, Perth and Stirling), accelerating schedules, providing more seats and more comfort (plus a 'real' catering service for the first time in many years) on key routes. The

ScotRail's modernised HST fleet will be based at Haymarket depot in Edinburgh and, from May 2019, it will link Scotland's seven cities via an improved inter-city network. On April 15, 2018, power cars Nos. 43148 and 43033 proudly display their new livery at Haymarket during staff training. PAUL SMITH

porterbrook

Wabtec Brush in Loughborough is overhauling 54 power cars for ScotRail. Work includes corrosion repairs, electrical modifications and a striking new livery. On June 19, 2018, No. 43032 shows signs of bodywork repairs as it is prepared for its new life. BEN JONES

The 2+4 formation GWR 'Castle' sets have a very high power-to-weight ratio with 4500hp on tap – making them an 'HST GTi' ideal for reducing journey times on a challenging route with frequent stops. From May 2019 they will help GWR to double the frequency of services between Plymouth and Penzance to half-hourly. On March 19, 2018, Nos. 43016 and 43093 power an Exeter-Truro test run near St Germans in Cornwall. BARRY JONES

first ex-GWR sets have been in Scotland since September 2017 for driver and depot training, while the first modified and reliveried power car headed north in early-February. Unfortunately, the refurbished and modernised Mk3 trailers were not delivered by Wabtec in time for the trains to make their Scottish debut in May 2018. Four refurbished 2+4 HSTs should have been introduced on the Edinburgh-Aberdeen route at the May 2018 timetable change. However, ScotRail is still hopeful that the first sets will be introduced later this year, with phased introductions through to May 2019.

HIGHER QUALITY

Currently, long-distance passengers are expected to travel between the Central Belt and the likes of Aberdeen, Dundee and Inverness in two or three-car Class 158 and Class 170 sets that are unsuitable for high-profile inter-city work. As far back as 2014, Transport

Scotland discussed how to change that and the Scottish Government was eager for any new franchise to include that step-change in quality. When Abellio won the deal in 2015, it confirmed that HSTs were part of its plan.

Before entering use with ScotRail, the HSTs are undergoing an extensive refurbishment, as well as modifications to ensure they meet PRM-TSI accessibility rules – enabling them to stay in traffic beyond December 31, 2019.

Wabtec's Brush Traction works in Loughborough is overhauling 54 Class 43 power cars owned by Angel Trains, while Wabtec Rail in Doncaster is refurbishing and modernising 121 Mk 3 trailer cars. Work includes corrosion repairs, the installation of forward-facing CCTV cameras and electrical modifications to add a traction interlocking system preventing trains from departing a station until the power-operated doors are locked.

Vaper Stone power-operated single-leaf doors with Wilee door control systems are being fitted in place of the slam

doors on the Mk3s. Doors will be interlocked with the driving controls and there will be a temporary override plunger and permanent isolation switch in the cab.

Nine four-coach and 17 five-car sets will be produced, each with 32 First Class and 206 Standard Class seats in the four-car sets and 278 seats in the five-car trains. This will deliver a 30% increase in seating capacity over existing DMUs, says ScotRail.

The sliding doors are the same design as those being fitted to CrossCountry's five HSTs and 11 GWR 'Castle' 2+4 HST sets for the West Country. ScotRail has worked with the other operators to gain approval from the Office of Rail and Road (ORR). Rolling stock owner Angel Trains has managed the project, while ASR will oversee the introduction of the trains into traffic.

In Standard Class, the same seats as those fitted to ScotRail Class 158 DMUs Nos. 158701-725 will be installed. Seats will have flip-down tables and armrests and the seats will align with windows, allowing passengers to enjoy the scenic views.

Seats will have the same pitch as ScotRail's Class 170s, which is greater than the 1680mm pitch on GWR HST sets. Controlled-emission toilets are also being fitted, including one accessible

On April 11, 2018, the first GWR 'Castle' set passes Dawlish with the 06.00 Penzance to Exeter St Davids, formed of power cars Nos. 43016 and 43187 and modernised Mk3 trailers Nos. 48101, 48102, 48111 and 49101. DAVID HUNT

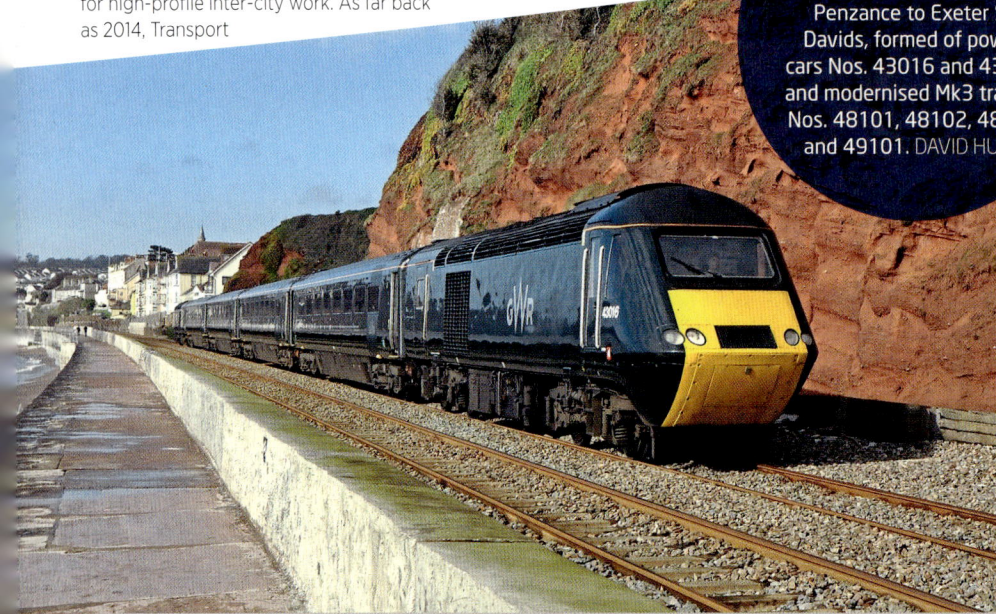

porterbrook

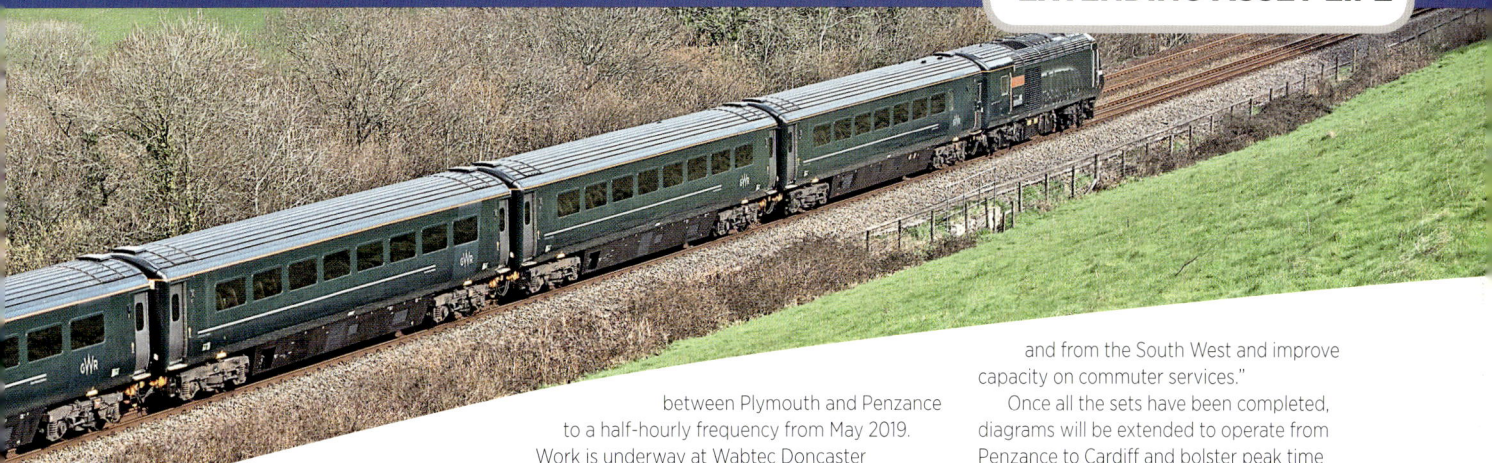

toilet per train and three additional toilets per five-coach set, or two extra in a four-car set.

The HSTs will be based at Haymarket depot in Edinburgh, which has been extensively modernised to accommodate the trains, and their differing requirements from underfloor engine DMUs. Servicing will also take place at Aberdeen, Inverness, Perth and Eastfield in Glasgow.

They may be around 40 years old, but ScotRail's new HSTs look set to deliver a much better experience for ScotRail's inter-city passengers, with shorter journeys, more seats, a better view and a quieter ride than the current diesel units.

GREEN FLEET

Meanwhile, a long way from Scotland, a similar project to re-use surplus HST vehicles is unfolding in the West Country. Although it is gradually releasing the trains from front-line duties radiating from Paddington, Great Western Railway has opted to retain 11 short-formation sets to improve long-distance semi-fast services between Bristol, Exeter and Penzance.

The 2+4 formation 'Castle' sets will replace Class 15x 'Sprinter' sets, providing a significant increase in passenger comfort and helping to boost services

between Plymouth and Penzance to a half-hourly frequency from May 2019.

Work is underway at Wabtec Doncaster to convert former 2+8 HSTs into refurbished Standard Class-only 'Castle' sets. GWR will retain 48 Mk3 trailers and 24 power cars to form 11 sets, with four spare vehicles. With 316 seats, a 'Castle' set will have more than twice as many seats as a two-car Class 150 DMU.

Slam doors will be replaced with power-operated sliding doors, controlled emission toilets and an improved passenger information system. A total of 35 Trailer Seconds (Nos. 48101-135) and 13 Trailer Guards Standard (Nos. 49101-113) are being modified for the new service.

GWR commercial development director Matthew Golton said of the 'Castle' sets: "These trains will replace smaller, less powerful trains in the West Country, doubling the number of seats, as part of our commitment to improving rolling stock across every part of the GWR network.

"They will work alongside the new Intercity Express Trains from summer 2019, helping us to double the frequency of services to

and from the South West and improve capacity on commuter services."

Once all the sets have been completed, diagrams will be extended to operate from Penzance to Cardiff and bolster peak time services between Gloucester and Taunton.

The 'Castle' sets will be maintained at GWR's Laira depot in Plymouth, which has been associated with the HST fleet since the late-1970s. Servicing will also take place at Long Rock depot in Penzance.

In early-2018, the first modified set was put to work, replacing a DMU on a regular Exeter-Penzance diagram. More 'Castles' should have been introduced at the May 2018 timetable change, but GWR's sets are also affected by the delays experienced at Wabtec's Doncaster works, which have disrupted work to modernise Mk3 trailers for GWR, ScotRail and CrossCountry.

An artist's impression of a pair of ScotRail HSTs under the roof at Glasgow Queen Street, which is also being modernised and rebuilt to accommodate longer and more frequent trains.
SCOTRAIL

porterbrook

From Upminster to upcycled:
Vivarail's D-Train

This innovative company is converting redundant District Line trains to provide cheaper alternatives to brand new multiple units – and looking to the future with greener methods of propulsion.

porterbrook

Somewhere deep in rural Warwickshire, a former London Underground D Stock driving car stands on a railway siding. Surrounded by dozens of its sisters, mothballed Midland Metro tramcars, ex-Thameslink '319s' and redundant freight wagons, it's not much to look at. But suddenly and silently it sets off, accelerating quickly and cantering around the test track with no more than a distant electrical whine. No, it's not a runaway, but Vivarail's battery powered 'D-Train' demonstrator – one of several options the company is now developing to power its upcycled trains.

Inside, a bank of batteries obtained from the Bombardier/Network Rail Independently Powered Electric Multiple Unit (IPEMU) project provides power for the traction motors and enough charge for up to 80 hours of operation. While it's unlikely that this could be replicated in the harsher realities of main line operation, computer simulations predict that it would be sufficient for a full-day diagram on a branch line such as Maidenhead-Marlow.

The modular design of the company's traction packages is encouraging it to investigate various methods of propulsion, from diesel-electric 'gensets' to DC or AC electric, hybrids and, in the longer term, hydrogen fuel cells. The single-car battery prototype was developed in just four months, between January and April 2017, in response to the changing demands of train operators. The first production battery train is close to completion and should start its main line trials in April.

Since Vivarail's inception around five years ago, the UK rail market has changed rapidly. Initially envisaged as a way of reusing spare D Stock sets to solve a looming shortage of DMUs, and replace the Class 142-144 'Pacer' railbuses, the trains are now being offered as a potential 'green' alternative to conventional diesel units for urban and low-density rural routes.

CORROSION-FREE

Led by Chiltern Railways' chairman Adrian Shooter and former Wrexham & Shropshire Railway managing director Andy Hamilton, with financial backing from the Railroad Development Corporation (RRDC) in the US, Vivarail has acquired 228 vehicles from London Underground Ltd (LUL) – enough for around 70-75 'D-Trains'. With their corrosion-free aluminium bodies and relatively new FLEX100 bogies fitted during a refurbishment programme less than 10 years ago, the vehicles were seen as an ideal basis for 'upcycling' to create new main line trains.

The initial offer featured diesel-electric units with two 3.2l Ford diesel engine packs per driving car (each powering one bogie), linked to 'gensets' driving DC traction motors. Central to the concept is a highly modular underframe arrangement, allowing engine, battery or generator packs to be exchanged very quickly using a forklift truck – largely eliminating the need for depot visits. Vivarail claims that engine changes can be completed in just 10 minutes and that 'D-Trains' will only require inspections over a pit road every nine months. With most maintenance possible at the trackside, empty mileage to and from the depot can be reduced, cutting operating and fuel costs. The purchase price is reckoned to be around two-thirds that of a comparable new vehicle, although purchase and leasing costs of new trains have dropped over the last few years, while fuel consumption is also around a third less than with a conventional DMU.

Conversion includes stripping the bodyshell back to bare metal, the addition of strengthening sections in the cab to meet main line requirements, a complete rewire and extensive modification of the underframe to accommodate the new equipment. Modifications have also been made to the solebar to ensure the cars comply with Network Rail's gauging requirements. In theory, a 'D-Train' can run anywhere an ex-BR Class 15x 'Sprinter' can go – which is almost anywhere on the network.

Internally, rebuilt cabs, new LED lighting, door controls with selective door opening (SDO) and passenger information systems are fitted, along with new and/or refurbished seating in a variety of arrangements suited to metro, regional or rural operation, according to customer choice. A fully accessible toilet can also be fitted if required. The wide, single-piece sliding doors, wide vestibules and flat floors help to make the trains compliant with the new PRM-TSI accessibility regulations which come into force in 2020.

Sporadic main line testing has been underway since late-2016 with prototype set No. 230001 restarted in spring 2018 on the Cotswold Line. Plans for a passenger trial with London Midland on the Coventry-Nuneaton line were scuppered by a widely-publicised fire in December 2016, which

June saw Transport for Wales and its development partner for the new Wales & Borders franchise, KeolisAmey, order five three-car diesel/battery hybrid trains for use in North Wales. The fleet will enter service in May 2019. TRANSPORT FOR WALES

Cymru a'r Gororau Wales & Borders

porterbrook

No. 230002 is the first production 'D-Train' with battery propulsion, featuring numerous modifications and improvements over the prototype set. A single car test vehicle was fitted with equipment acquired from the Bombardier/Network Rail Class 379 IPEMU project, and formed the basis of development work into battery and hybrid 'D-Trains'. BEN JONES

damaged one of the train's driving cars. The cause of the fire was traced to a fuel leak in one of the power packs, and to the positioning of the fuel cut-off device on the opposite side of the engine to the fuel inlet. The power packs have now been redesigned, based on the conclusions of Vivarail's investigation, and two fire protection systems are now fitted, allowing trains to continue running on one engine and limiting damage to one power pack.

Testing with No. 230001 has also allowed the company to modify and improve the design for its production trains. DC traction motors have been replaced by AC equipment and a new design of genset produced by Strukton in the Netherlands has been introduced on No. 230002.

This first production train features the so-called 'City' interior with Underground-style longitudinal seating but will also, for the first time, feature new gangways between cars.

Various other design and production improvements have been identified, including the in-house assembly of diesel power packs. In December 2017, Vivarail announced that it is opening a new production facility in Seaham, Co. Durham, a location chosen to take advantage of the region's highly-skilled labour pool and engineering base. Up to £100,000 will be invested in the 11,000sq ft production site. Three different types of powerpack will be assembled at the new plant, including diesel gensets and a pioneering

Prototype 'D-Train' No. 230001 stands in the sun at Quinton Rail Technology Centre on November 6. Vivarail says this train has done its job by providing vital operational experience and identifying areas where the train's design can be improved. BEN JONES

230001

porterbrook

battery-only system currently being developed with £640,000 grant funding awarded in 2017 by Innovate UK. The site could also be expanded to refurbish other components, such as the bogies, if demand grows as hoped. Up to 30 jobs could eventually be created in Seaham, in addition to the 50 people already employed by the company.

ORDERS

Since the concept was first revealed in 2014, Vivarail has reported keen interest from train operators and leasing companies, but received no firm orders until March 2018, when Abellio confirmed its intention to take three two-car diesel sets from December for London Northwestern's Bedford-Bletchley route. That was followed in June by an order for five diesel-battery hybrid three-car trains from Transport for Wales/KeolisAmey.

In both cases, the '230s' will be the first 'new' trains to be introduced by franchises that have recently changed hands. Production of the LNR sets is well underway and the first set should be delivered shortly. TfW's trains will make their debut in March to May 2019 on the Conwy Valley line in North Wales, releasing Class 15x DMUs to provide additional capacity in South Wales. The small hybrid fleet will be based at a purpose-built depot in Wrexham and will also work the Wrexham-Bidston route.

The TfW trains will have battery packs installed in the driving cars and four diesel gensets under the middle vehicle. Regenerative braking will recover much of the kinetic energy from braking to replenish the batteries, reducing fuel consumption by up to 20%.

Welcoming the TfW order, Adrian Shooter said:

"This is a very exciting day for us and we are proud to be supplying the first of the new trains for Wales.

"We know that KeolisAmey want to bring the best new trains to their passengers so our interior layout has been designed to do exactly that. "As well as the wide and spacious carriages, the trains will have a Universal Access Toilet, wi-fi, air-conditioning, USB ports and power sockets. There will be a range of seating layouts and plenty of space for bikes and luggage.

"Our aim has always been to provide innovative solutions for operators and to that end I'm delighted that our trains will be built as battery/diesel hybrids to cut down on emissions. With this hybrid fleet we will deliver a train that is clean, green and reliable, making use of GPS systems to cut out the engines in stations and environmentally-sensitive areas."

Elsewhere, political and public reaction has been mixed, with strong criticism from some commentators, particularly in northern England, who are hostile to more 'hand-me-downs' from London and others questioning the suitability of the 60mph trains for the longer-distance regional services operating across the north. Vivarail's hopes of providing 'Pacer' replacements to the new Northern franchise were dashed in December 2015 when Arriva elected to buy new DMUs from CAF in Spain.

The builder says that for 95% of the routes it has modelled for 'D-Train' operation, the faster acceleration and shorter station stops possible with the train compensates for its lower top speed. It also argues that many regional and local trains rarely manage 60mph between stops with the current trains.

However, there has been interest in the trains

for rural lines in south-west England and from the promoters of reopening schemes keen to keep costs as low as possible. Vivarail says it is talking to various potential customers, but will not reveal their identity until contracts are signed.

According to the company, up to two or three trains can be completed per month at its Long Marston base. A production plan is in place through to the end of 2019, aimed at providing vehicles to meet the looming PRM-TSI deadline. Should the concept take off even further, Vivarail says it will be in the market for more suitable vehicles to convert and, in the longer term, it could look at building all-new vehicles using the technology pioneered on No. 230001 and battery demonstrator No. 230002.

With conventional electrification falling out of favour and the Department for Transport (DfT) encouraging operators to look at cleaner sources of energy for self-propelled trains, attention has switched to battery and hydrogen technology. Vivarail is working with BOC, Ballard and AirTech to develop hydrogen fuel cells suitable for the 'D-Train', but it is also considering numerous ways to make battery-powered EMUs a reality, including recharging from banks of recycled car batteries at strategic points such as branch termini. Drawing power from overhead catenary at electrified main line stations, or short sections of OLE installed purely for charging purposes, is also suggested as a realistic option.

In the short-term, diesel-battery hybrids are likely to offer a 'belt-and-braces' compromise, especially in a conservative railway market where no one wants to be the first to adopt unproven technology. While Porterbrook has secured orders from Northern and Arriva Trains Wales for its bi-mode Class 319 'Flex' electro-diesel multiple units (EDMUs), Vivarail is looking at different markets for its trains, providing new, lower-cost options for both urban and rural transport in the coming years.

porterbrook

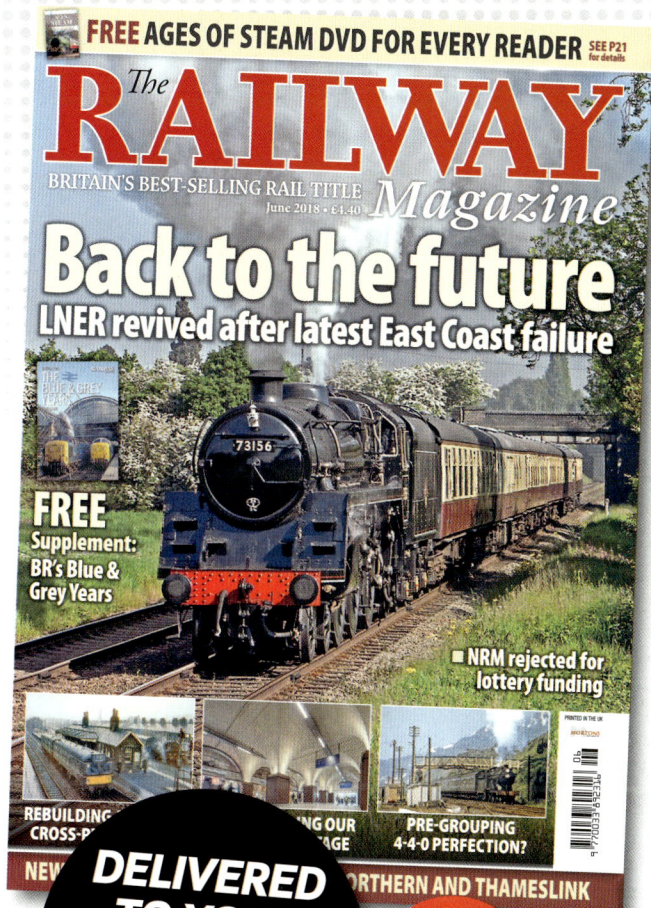

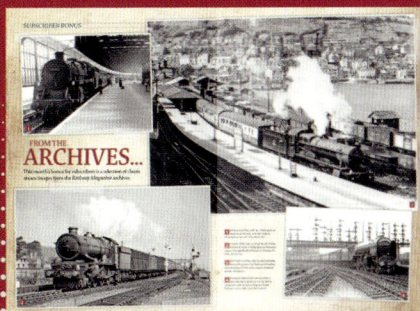

Moving

The introduction of thousands of new passenger vehicles raises the question of what to do with the current fleets. Over the last few years, operators, leasing companies and the Department for Transport have been working on a hugely complex series of cascades to modernise and expand train fleets across the country.

An increasingly familiar sight on the modern railway: Rail Operations Group No. 47812 passes Wistow in Leicestershire while moving two off-lease Class 319 EMUs from Cricklewood to Long Marston on January 24, 2017. RAILWAY MAGAZINE ARCHIVE

porterbrook

On

While many of the new trains being delivered are intended to increase capacity on key routes, others have been ordered to replace existing trains, many of which date back to the British Rail (BR) era. Since the earliest days of railways, trains displaced from front-line service have often been cascaded to less arduous or lower-profile duties – for example moving from London commuter lines to rural lines in northern England, the West Country or Scotland.

The huge number of new trains now being produced, coupled with the much more complex ownership arrangements of the privatised railway, has resulted in an enormously convoluted programme of cascades, which will see hundreds of existing trains move to new operators. Rolling Stock Owning Companies (ROSCOs) such as Porterbrook, Eversholt and Angel Trains are keen to ensure the continued use of these valuable assets, many of which have received (or are scheduled to receive) expensive refurbishment programmes to allow them to meet current standards.

Earlier this decade, when a rolling programme of electrification was expected, it was thought that the younger ex-BR EMUs would move to pastures new as more routes were wired. However, the curtailment of the GW Main Line programme, and cancellation of other schemes on the Midland Main Line, in South Wales and northern England have created a headache for the ROSCOs. The recent trend towards massive new train orders, encouraged by low purchase and leasing costs, has also disrupted the traditional flow of cascades.

LIFE BEGINS AT 40

Despite their age, some of the InterCity 125s being displaced by IETs have had no problem finding new homes. GWR is retaining 11 modernised 'Castle' sets for regional services in the West Country. Formed into shortened 2+4 sets with extensively rebuilt Mk 3 trailers, modified with power-operated sliding doors, they will be based in Penzance and are expected to enter service from late-2018. GWR is retaining power cars

porterbrook

EXTENDING ASSET LIFE

An early-2018 scene that has already changed as new fleets take over East Coast Main Line duties. LNER is replacing all but six IC225 sets with new Class 801 Intercity Express Trains and Great Northern has returned 19 Class 365s to Eversholt after the introduction of Thameslink Class 700s. BEN JONES

ScotRail is currently training staff to drive and maintain InterCity 125s ahead of their introduction on its new 'InterCity 7' network linking Scotland's largest cities. By May 2019, 27 short-formed IC125 sets will have replaced Class 158 and 170 DMUs, providing higher-quality and faster services. SCOTRAIL

Nos. 43005/024/040-042/092-094/097/098, 43122/153-155/158/170/172/186-189/192/194/198.

To improve its domestic InterCity services, Abellio ScotRail is introducing 27 short-formed HST sets. The first set should have entered service on the Edinburgh-Aberdeen route in May, but delays to the refurbished coaching stock have seen this deferred until later in 2018. The whole fleet should be in traffic by May 2019.

Fifty-four overhauled ex-GWR power cars and 121 refurbished Mk 3 trailers with new power-operated sliding doors and high-quality interiors will be formed into 17 2+4 and nine 2+5 sets to work between Edinburgh, Glasgow,

Aberdeen and Inverness. They will replace ASR Class 170s, some of which are being cascaded to Arriva Northern, while others will allow trains to be lengthened on other routes in Scotland. ASR Nos. 170453-461/472-478 will move south by December. Some entered service with Northern on the Harrogate-Leeds line in May. Electrification also allowed ASR to release eight Class 158s (158782/786/789/867-872) to Northern in January.

ENGLISH INTER-CITY

Of the 30 InterCity 225 sets currently used by LNER (Class 91+9xMk4+DVT), six to eight shortened sets are expected to be retained for Anglo-Scottish

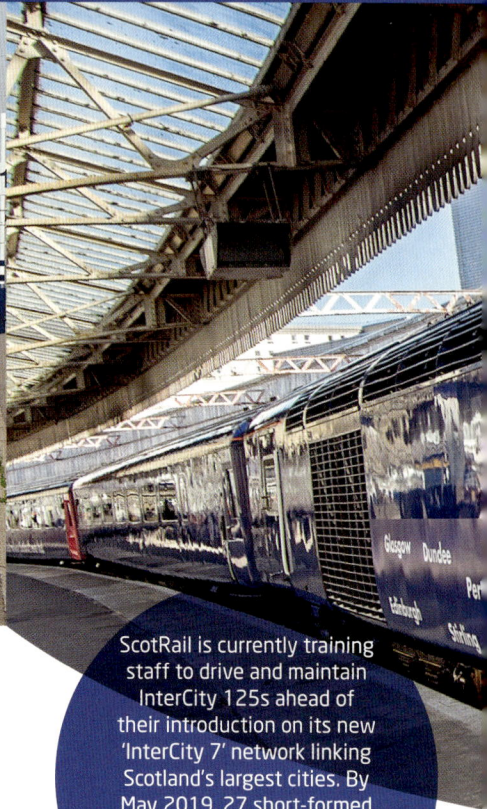

A glimpse of a possible redeployment of South Western Railway's Class 707 fleet as Nos. 707001/002 pass Farringdon during test runs to assess the type's performance on 25kv AC overhead supply in late-2017. Set to become spare after SWR introduces new Class 701s in 2020-21, a transfer to 25kv AC routes north of the Thames could be one option for these nearly new trains. EIKI SEKINE

porterbrook

duties and Alliance Rail is expected to take on five sets formed of a Class 91, six Mk 4s and a DVT (plus a spare '91') for its new 'Great North Western Railway' Euston-Blackpool open access operation. Wales & Borders is also taking 12 Mk 4 coaches and three DVTs from December 2019 for its Cardiff-Holyhead services (see below).

GWR's new bi-mode trains allowed the operator's remaining Class 180 five-car DMUs to join their sisters at First Hull Trains and Grand Central in late-2017. The latter replaced its own HSTs with Class 180s in December 2017 and the power cars and Mk 3s have moved to East Midlands Trains to create additional capacity and operational flexibility. The longer-term future of the Hull Trains '180s' is uncertain, as the open access operator will introduce five Hitachi bi-mode Class 802s to replace them in December 2019.

Electrification in the Thames Valley is allowing GWR to move some of its Class 165/166 'Networker' DMUs west to work around Bristol and Exeter. In turn, they are displacing Class 150s to Northern. Eventually, all 50 Class 150/1s will be united in the Northern fleet, including three released by London Northwestern (Nos. 150105/107/109) from the Bedford-Bletchley route and replaced by three two-car Class 230s from December 2018.

The '150' fleet is steadily being refurbished and fitted with accessible toilets to keep it in traffic for the foreseeable future. Much of the fleet will eventually be concentrated with Northern. Wales & Borders Class 150/2s are undergoing modifications to make them compliant with new PRM-TSI rules and will be retained as part of the Transport for Wales (TfW) regional fleet until they are replaced at the end of 2023.

TransPennine Express (TPE) is transforming its fleet over the next couple of years and while it will retain 29 Class 185s for the Manchester Airport-Sheffield-Cleethorpes route, 22 sets will be released, possibly to Northern. More may also be retained if the Department for Transport decides to hand control of Liverpool-Manchester-Sheffield-Nottingham inter-urban services to TPE or Northern when the East Midlands franchise is reorganised later this year.

Also on the move are London Overground's eight Class 172/0 DMUs. Nos. 172001-008 are due to join their Class 172/1 cousins in the West Midlands after electric operation starts on the Gospel Oak-Barking line in November.

Abellio's new London Northwestern Railway (LNR) franchise will receive all 10 four-car Class 350/4 EMUs (Nos. 350401-410) from TransPennine Express in 2019, boosting its 'Desiro' fleet ahead of the introduction of the new Bombardier 'Aventra' Class 731/732 sets in 2021.

REGIONAL MOVES

The massive Class 700 EMU order has transformed the Thameslink operation over the last couple of years, displacing many Class 319s to Northern and allowing newer Class 377/387 'Electrostars' to move to Southern and Southeastern. Many other Class 319s are now in secure storage at locations such as Long Marston in Warwickshire awaiting new operators or conversion into bi-mode electro-diesel trains.

Porterbrook has commissioned Wabtec/Brush to modify some of its Class 319s as electro-diesel Class 769 'Flex' trains able to work away from the wires on routes such as Manchester Airport-Windermere and in South Wales. May 2018 should have seen Northern introduce the first of eight Class 769s, but the project has experienced delays. Testing started at the Great Central Railway in July and was expected to move to the main line in late-summer with a view to the first sets entering service in late-2018. Five '769s' are also destined for Wales & Borders, while GWR has also ordered 19 tri-mode 'Flex' sets capable of working on 750v DC third-rail, 25kv AC overhead and on diesel.

The new Wales & Borders franchise starting in October will be the catalyst for another major reorganisation of train fleets. During 2019, five Class 769s, five ex-GWR Class 153s and 12 Class 170 DMUs (eight three-car and four two-car sets released by Greater Anglia) will join the Wales & Borders fleet as an interim measure. For the thrice-daily Cardiff-Holyhead service, three shortened and refurbished sets of Mk 4 stock (four passenger coaches plus DVT) released by LNER will replace the current Mk 3 sets in December 2019.

The fleet changes will mean that Class 142/143 'Pacers' and Mk 3 stock will be eliminated by the end of 2019, with the Class 153s, 158s and Class 175s – and the yet-to-be-seen Class 769s – all going during 2022. The Class 150/2 fleet, which is currently

The announcement that the new Wales & Borders operator is to procure a new fleet of Welsh-built CAF DMUs for regional routes has put the long-term future of the Alstom Class 175s in doubt. However, with demand for good quality DMUs still strong, they are likely to find new homes after 2022.
BEN JONES

being refurbished to meet new PRM-TSI accessibility rules, is expected to continue until the end of 2023.

One fleet with which the future is still fluid is the Class 153 diesel railcars. The 70 single-car trains are currently used by East Midlands Trains, West Midlands Railway, Arriva Trains Wales (Wales & Borders from October), GWR, Greater Anglia and Arriva Rail North, with ownership split between Angel Trains and Porterbrook. The difficulties of fitting much larger accessible toilet cubicles into these trains, reducing capacity, led many to believe that their days were numbered after December 2019. However, several options are now being considered to prolong their lives, including reuniting them as two-car Class 155s (they were rebuilt into single cars by Regional Railways in 1991/92), adding them to other Class 15x DMUs to create semi-permanent three-car (or longer) trains and rebuilding them as luggage/cycle vans for scenic routes.

Abellio ScotRail is planning to take five '153s' in 2019 and couple them to Class 156s used on the West Highland Line, creating extra capacity and providing space for luggage, cycles and bulky sports equipment on this popular tourist route. If successful, the idea could be rolled out on the Oban, Kyle of Lochalsh and Far North lines.

Over the next couple of years WMR,

GA and GWR will hand back their allocations, leaving East Midlands and Northern as the probable long-term operators after Wales & Borders returns its '153s' in 2022.

ELECTRIC SUPPLY

ScotRail has taken seven Class 321s from Greater Anglia and London Midland, reducing them to three cars to create additional Class 320s (Nos. 320411-417) for Strathclyde area suburban routes. One surprising, but very welcome, return is the modernisation and refurbishment of 18 Class 442 'Wessex Electric' EMUs (see page 96) by South Western Railway (SWR). Fitted with new Vossloh Kiepe traction packages to replace their second-hand (ex-'4-REP') English Electric equipment, the revamped trains should be introduced on the Waterloo-Portsmouth route in late-2018. The other six '442s' could also return to use, with new open access operator Alliance Rail on the Waterloo-Southampton route.

Originally destined for the Thames Valley, Great Northern returned 19 of the 41 Class 365s to Eversholt in the first half of 2018 after the widespread introduction of Thameslink Class 700s and Class 387s on the King's Cross-Cambridge-King's Lynn/Peterborough routes. Ten units subsequently went on short-term lease to ScotRail as cover for delayed Class 385s, allowing Class 170s to be cascaded south, but the future for these well-regarded EMUs remains unclear.

Even relatively new trains such as Greater Anglia's Class 360/1s (21 four-car sets) and the

Heathrow Connect Class 360/2s (five five-car sets) will be replaced by newer trains in the next two years.

Two other modern EMU fleets set to become surplus to requirements are London Northwestern's Siemens Class 350/2s (Nos. 350231-267), which will be replaced by new Bombardier 'Aventras' in 2020/21, and Greater Anglia's 30 four-car Class 379 'Electrostars' – used on the Liverpool Street-Stansted/Cambridge route. The latter will be ousted by Stadler 'FLIRT UK' and 'Aventra' EMUs from 2020. No new customers have yet been confirmed

porterbrook

A changing scene at London Paddington on June 1. Hitachi IETs are already replacing GWR's HST fleet on long-distance diagrams, while many of GWR's Class 165/166 DMUs are being cascaded to the West Country after replacement by Class 387 EMUs. From 2019, dedicated Heathrow Express Class 332s will be replaced by GWR 387s modified for airport duties. BEN JONES

by the owners of these expensive and sophisticated modern trains.

However, industry sources suggest that Porterbrook's 110mph Class 350/2s, Britain's most reliable passenger train fleet over the last few years, could be the leading contender for the London-Corby route when electric operation starts in December 2019. The 37 four-car trains are currently configured for 3+2 suburban seating, but could be reseated for outer suburban or even long-distance work, depending on their destination. Options are also being investigated to cascade them to TSGN or another West Coast Main Line operator.

From 2020, South Western Railway's Bombardier-built Class 701s will replace 97 ex-BR Class 455s (many recently fitted with new traction packages), 24 two-car Class 456s, 36 five-car Class 485s and even the 30 nearly-new Siemens Class 707s that entered passenger service in December 2017!

Porterbrook has stated that the re-tractioned Class 455s are a candidate for rebuilding as bi-mode 'Flex' trains once they become spare. Some of these surplus trains will almost certainly find new homes, probably elsewhere on the former Southern Region network, but others are destined for storage and possibly the scrapyard.

Below: Wabtec/Brush in Loughborough is refurbishing 54 ex-GWR Class 43 power cars for Abellio ScotRail. Work includes corrosion repairs and electrical modifications to allow them to work with Mk 3 trailers fitted with new power-operated sliding doors. No. 43125 is prepared for its new life at the Brush Falcon Works on June 28. BEN JONES

Turn over for more information on the train fleets reaching the end of their careers and possible options for further use.

porterbrook

End of the line

By the end of 2019, this view at Manchester Piccadilly will have changed completely as Northern withdraws all of its 'Pacer' railbuses and the Class 323 EMUs are replaced by new CAF Class 331s on Greater Manchester suburban duties. Neither fleet looks likely to find new employment elsewhere on the network. RAILWAY MAGAZINE ARCHIVE

porterbrook

While some new train fleets are intended to increase capacity, others will replace life-expired vehicles dating from the 1970s and 1980s. However, the sheer volume of new trains means that even some trains that could still perform a useful function could go for scrap in the next few years.

London Paddington

A classic view that has been possible at London Paddington since 1976, but will soon be consigned to history. A line-up of Great Western Railway (ex-FGW) High Speed Trains waiting for their next westbound dash at Paddington on June 1. BEN JONES

The oldest passenger trains currently in regular use are the 1970s 'PEP' generation trains of Classes 313-315/507/508, dating from the second half of the 1970s. Great Northern's Class 313s, introduced in 1976, will be replaced by new Derby-built Class 717s from December 2018 and ScotRail says its 14 Class 314 three-car sets will be retired by the end of this year as more Hitachi Class 385s become available.

By December 2019, Crossrail will be fully operational, releasing TfL Rail's Class 315s from the Shenfield route, and their sisters, currently working for London Overground, will be replaced by new Class 710 'Aventras' after 40 years of loyal service on Liverpool Street inner-suburban duties. Plans to cascade some of the '315s' to South Wales to work the Cardiff Valleys lines were superseded by the Government's cancellation of South Wales electrification schemes and, more recently, the Welsh Government's ambitious South Wales Metro plans (see page 82).

From 2020, Merseyrail's Class 507s and 508s will become surplus to requirements as the new Stadler Class 777 EMUs enter service. That will leave a fleet of just 20 ex-GN Class 313s in use

on Southern's 'Coastway' routes from Brighton – but for how long? With a large number of more modern electric units coming onto the market in the next three years, there will be no shortage of offers to replace them.

Also on their way out are the widely-disliked Class 142-144 'Pacers', employed by Northern, GWR and Arriva Trains Wales. The first Northern Class 142s are set to go off-lease in September and will gradually disappear from the north of England as new and cascaded DMUs arrive to replace them. Although Porterbrook had

> " The first Northern 'Pacers' will go off-lease in September and will be gradually retired until the last sets are released back to their owners in October 2019. "

hoped to prolong the life of the '144s' with its 'Evolution' concept, tested on No. 144012, they also appear to be destined for retirement.

The first Northern 'Pacers' will go off-lease on September 15, with the final trains expected to be released on October 12, 2019.

First to be released will be five two-car Class 144s owned by Porterbrook. The final

two-car '144s' will be withdrawn on January 5, 2019, while the 10 three-car '144s' (Nos. 144014-023) will be released on March 31, 2019.

The future of ATW's Class 142s and 143s has been sealed by Transport for Wales (TfW) and all will be withdrawn by the end of 2019. Although new Stadler FLIRTs and 'CityLink' tram-trains are not due until 2021-23, GWR Class 153s and

ex-Greater Anglia Class 170s are being drafted in to hasten their demise. Likewise, GWR's Class 143s will survive until they are replaced by cascaded Class 165/166s around Bristol and Exeter in 2019.

Angel Trains and Porterbrook, the Rolling Stock Companies (ROSCOs) that own the 'Pacers', are understandably keen for their assets to continue earning revenue, rather than heading

porterbrook

One of the more surprising moves of 2018 was the announcement that GWR is to take over Heathrow Express services, replacing the dedicated CAF/Siemens Class 332s with modified Class 387s. This will leave the 1997/98-built fleet without work and facing an uncertain future. BEN JONES

to the scrapyard.

Various ideas have been mooted, including retaining some trains as peak time 'crowd-busters' (with toilets removed to avoid having to install PRM-TSI compliant accessible cubicles) or as additional capacity for luggage, cycles and sports equipment on scenic routes. Export also remains an option, with many countries keen to obtain basic, simple-to-maintain passenger trains at a reasonable price.

TfW's total fleet replacement programme will also release 24 ex-BR Class 158s and the entire Alstom-built Class 175 DMU fleet (11 two-car and 16 three-car sets), dating from 1999-2001. Although no destination has yet been announced, it would be a surprise if these high-quality 90mph DMUs did not find a new home.

HSTs UNDER THREAT

While GWR and ScotRail have made headlines by introducing shortened InterCity 125 sets, much of the fleet remains at risk, particularly those not being updated to meet new PRM-TSI rules in force from January 1, 2020. CrossCountry is also investing in updating its HST fleet to allow it to continue beyond December 2019.

Although the new Southeastern franchise covering south-east London and Kent is not announced until later this year, it is widely expected that it will involve new trains to replace some or all of the current fleet. 'Networker' EMU No. 465196 and inner-suburban 'Electrostar' No. 376030 call at London Bridge on June 1. BEN JONES

However, more than 100 Class 43 power cars owned by Angel Trains and Porterbrook and hundreds of Mk 3 trailer vehicles will be rendered surplus by the introduction of new Intercity Express Trains (IETs) by GWR and LNER in 2018-20. That total also includes 11 Porterbrook HSTs (24 power cars, 84 trailers) currently leased to East Midlands Trains and due to be withdrawn by December 2019. Controversially, no trains have yet been ordered to replace them, and it's now very unlikely that they could be modernised before the looming deadline. No alternative solution has yet been revealed to fill the gap on MML inter-city services between

Former Heathrow Connect (now TfL Rail) 'Desiro' No. 360204 passes Royal Oak in west London with a Hayes & Harlington-Paddington local service on June 1. This small fleet of modern Siemens-built EMUs will be redundant once Elizabeth Line (Crossrail) starts operating the stopping service to Heathrow Airport in 2019. BEN JONES

A large number of existing EMUs will be spare once Greater Anglia's new fleet is in place. As well as ex-BR Class 317s and 321s of the 1980s, the 21 Siemens 'Desiro' Class 360/1s (built 2002/03) and 30 Bombardier Class 379s (built 2010/11) are looking for new homes. No. 360118 arrives at Stratford on June 1. BEN JONES

December 2019 and the delivery of the promised bi-mode trains in 2022/23. GB Railfreight is interested in using rebuilt ex-LNER HSTs for high-speed freight duties on main line routes, with Mk 3 trailers modified to carry high-value parcels and small consignments for courier companies. It remains to be seen whether this proposal is viable, but it could provide a new career for a small number of trains.

Another high-quality 125mph fleet at some risk is LNER's InterCity 225 (Class 91 + Mk 4) dating from the late-1980s and early-1990s. Under the previous franchise, Virgin Trains East Coast was expected to retain six IC225 sets for Anglo-Scottish services under the expanded timetable due in December 2019. However, with the infrastructure improvements to allow that enhanced service now delayed, LNER is likely to have more IETs than it requires. It remains to be seen whether the new operator-of-last-resort retains the older trains. Four or five shortened IC225 sets will also switch to new open access operator Great North Western Railway, but 20 Class 91s and 17 Mk 4 DVTs (three will go to TfW, along with 12 passenger coaches), plus around 180 Mk 4 passenger vehicles are currently waiting for new operators. In 2019/20, Greater Anglia will replace its

porterbrook

Porterbrook-owned
Class 90+Mk3 inter-city trains on the Liverpool Street-Norwich route with new 12-car Stadler 'FLIRT' EMUs. While it's possible that the 15 Class 90s will switch to freight work, possibly replacing Freightliner's 1965-vintage Class 86s, there is currently no plan to update the Mk3 passenger vehicles to meet new accessibility rules, allowing them to continue in service with another operator.

EMUs AT RISK

While it was always expected that the 1970s-built EMUs would be retired, the rolling programme of electrification announced earlier this decade was to have led to a cascade of electric trains built between the 1980s and 2000s away from London and the south-east of England to other parts of the country. Unfortunately, the Government's change of policy, favouring 'alternative fuels' and bi-mode trains over electrification, has cast doubt on the future of a large number of good quality electric units.

All 72 Class 317s (288 vehicles) dating from 1981-88 and currently operated by Greater Anglia and London Overground are at risk, as are Eversholt's 115 Class 321/322 EMUs of 1988-91 (460 vehicles). The GA sets will be replaced by new Class 720 Aventras from 2019 onwards. Despite the 'Renatus' project, which involves the extensive refurbishment of up to 30 Class 321/3s with new interiors and seating, the original plan to rebuild the trains with modern AC traction equipment (No. 321303 was converted as a prototype) was superseded by GA's decision to replace its entire fleet with new trains. Northern's Class 321s and 322s will also become surplus after new CAF EMUs are introduced in West Yorkshire.

However, Eversholt is working with Alstom to convert a Class 321 into an experimental hydrogen-powered testbed. If successful, this could provide a lifeline for many '321s' over the coming years, especially if combined with Eversholt's 'Renatus' modernisation.

GA's total fleet replacement will also make its 21 four-car Siemens-built Class 360/1s and 30 Class 379s redundant. No new homes have yet been found for either fleet, although the '379s' could join one of several other operators using 'Electrostars', or move to the new East Midlands franchise for the

Corby route, which goes over to electric operation at the end of 2019.

The same issue faces the six Heathrow Connect (now TfL Rail) Class 360/2s, which will be made redundant by the new Elizabeth Line service to Heathrow Airport. Their CAF/Siemens stablemates, the 14 Class 332s, will also be usurped from their Heathrow Express duties by modified GWR Class 387s in 2019 and currently face an uncertain future.

An uncertain future also faces the early-1990s Class 323 suburban units used in Greater Manchester and the West Midlands. It was originally intended to bring the 43-strong fleet together in Birmingham, once Northern's new CAF EMUs were delivered, but Abellio's order for new metro-style 'Aventras' in late-2017 renders them redundant.

The recent trend towards massive fleet replacement orders by new franchises has also cast a shadow over several other fleets, notably those currently operated by South Western Railway (SWR) and West Midlands Railway (WMR). SWR's 91 Class 455 four-car suburban sets, 24 two-car Class 456s and 36 five-car Class 458s (all owned by Porterbrook) are all at risk, although there is a suggestion that some of the Class 455s could be rebuilt as bi-mode electro-diesel trains, similar to the Class 769 'Flex' units (former Class 319s). Although SWR's nearly-new Siemens Class 707s are also being replaced, it seems unlikely that these modern commuter trains will not be re-homed.

The 43 Class 323 three-car EMUs currently used by Arriva Rail North and WMR will all be replaced over the next four years by new CAF and Bombardier trains and do not currently have a new home. Although 10 sets found a short-term role in Scotland from June 23, 21 Class 365s are also currently spare, having

Having taken delivery of 17 Siemens 'Velaro' Class 374 EMUs over the last few years, Eurostar is withdrawing its unrefurbished Class 373 'Three Capitals' high-speed trains dating from the mid-1990s. A small fleet of refurbished e300 sets is being retained for services away from the core London-Paris/Brussels/Amsterdam route, but the rest are being scrapped in the UK. BEN JONES

been released by Great Northern in 2018.

The new Southeastern franchise, due to start in December 2018, is also expected to include a major fleet replacement element, potentially putting the Class 465 and 466 'Networker' EMUs, built in the early-1990s, out of work. If the new franchisee follows SWR's example and opts for a uniform fleet of new trains, the 36 five-car Class 376 inner-suburban 'Electrostars', introduced in 2004, could also be difficult to place with another operator.

Finally, all but eight Eurostar Class 373s will be scrapped (several have already been disposed of) after the international operator introduced 20 new Siemens-built Class 374s for London-Paris/Brussels/Amsterdam services. The trains were originally to have been retained to allow for further expansion on routes such as London-Geneva but these plans have been shelved in recent years.

As can be seen from the list above, thousands of perfectly serviceable passenger vehicles will become redundant over the next few years. Unfortunately, the change in Government policy towards electrification means that as much as 60 miles of storage sidings will be required to accommodate around 5000 redundant vehicles over the coming years. Some will find new homes eventually, but many appear to be destined for the scrapyard unless a nationwide programme of electrification returns to the agenda in the near future.

NEW TRAINS FOR THE 2020s AND BEYOND

While High Speed 2 will continue to make headlines in the next decade and into the 2030s, the big train builders also have their eyes on numerous other major contracts for main line and mass transit operators in the UK.

Left: The proposed First Class interior of the Bombardier inter-city 'Aventra'. BOMBARDIER

Right: The proposed Standard Class interior of the Bombardier inter-city 'Aventra'. BOMBARDIER

porterbrook

Bombardier unveiled an inter-city version of its 'Aventra' family in the spring of 2018. Promising 125mph capability on electric or diesel power, with the option of battery power, it is aimed at winning orders for the next East Midlands, CrossCountry and West Coast franchises.
BOMBARDIER

porterbrook

> After many years out of the UK new train market, Alstom is once again bidding for contracts. Its product for the Greater Anglia and Midland Main Line contracts was the 'new EMU for the UK', although the Government's cancellation of the MML upgrade means that bi-mode trains will now be required.

T he sheer volume of new train orders in recent years has led many to conclude that the British rolling stock market is experiencing a 'bubble' that will inevitably burst before long. While it is true that the current rate of orders cannot be expected to continue, there remain a number of potentially lucrative contracts on the near horizon that the global transport companies would like to secure.

On the classic network, three large franchises are due to be re-let in late-2018 and 2019 – East Midlands, Southeastern and CrossCountry. Of those, East Midlands, which covers inter-city services from London St Pancras to the East Midlands and South Yorkshire has become the most controversial.

The Department for Transport (DfT) has already stated that the new operator will need to procure a new fleet of bi-mode trains capable of replacing the current High Speed Train fleet, which cannot continue in service beyond December 31, 2019. Those trains, which will utilise 25kv AC overhead supply south of Kettering and diesel power from there to Nottingham, Derby and Sheffield, will need to match the 'sports car' performance of a Bombardier Class 222 'Meridian' over a difficult route on which average speeds are limited by gradients, sharp curves and capacity issues.

Originally, the Midland Main Line (MML) was scheduled to be electrified throughout and a new fleet of electric inter-city trains would replace the HSTs and Class 222s in the early-2020s. Not only did the Government's cancellation

porterbrook

of that scheme cause huge controversy in the regions served by the MML, it threw a relatively simple fleet replacement plan into chaos.

Currently, no train exists to fulfil the DfT's requirements. Hitachi's AT300 (Class 800-802) was designed as an electric train with diesel power intended for relatively short distances away from the wires. While it can accelerate smartly away from stations, its performance on diesel is no match for a 40-year-old HST, let alone a 'Meridian' with a 750hp Cummins QSK19 engine under every car.

However, other suppliers are starting to show their hands with possible solutions to the MML problem. Bombardier, with its factory at the heart of the MML route in Derby, unveiled a bi-mode, inter-city variant of its 'Aventra' family in the spring of 2018. With an eye on the next CrossCountry and West Coast franchises, as well as East Midlands, the 125mph train would feature a higher-quality interior for inter-city work and doors at the ends of vehicles. Bombardier says the train could also be built to run on batteries rather than diesel engines, away from electrified routes and would be capable of 125mph operation in diesel mode, unlike Hitachi's Class 800 IETs, which were not designed for the sustained high-speed running on diesel to which they are now subjected. However, industry sources suggest that Hitachi could offer a new variant of its AT300 (Class 802) design, with additional diesel engines and shorter 24m vehicles, rather than the standard 26m, which are too long for the MML.

Another train-builder that could potentially supply inter-city bi-mode trains with enough 'oomph' to tackle the MML is Stadler. It is building a mix of electro-diesel regional and inter-city 'FLIRT' trains for Greater Anglia. GA's four-car Class 755/4s will feature a 2000hp articulated power pack, which should provide excellent performance. A 12-car inter-city 'FLIRT' fitted with these power packs could be an extremely capable high-performance train in both electric and diesel mode, or batteries could be fitted rather than diesel engines to allow cheaper, discontinuous electrification of the MML in the future.

Finally, CAF could be another contender for the MML new train contract with a bi-mode

variant of the Class 397 'Civity' 125mph EMU now being built for TransPennine Express.

The winner of the new East Midlands Railway franchise will be announced in April 2019 and will take over operation of the MML and regional routes across the East Midlands next August. Stagecoach, the current holder, is facing competition from Deutsche Bahn subsidiary Arriva and Abellio – a division of Netherlands Railways. Whichever company wins the race will face a challenging timetable to find a short-term replacement for its HSTs while the new bi-mode fleet is being designed and built for introduction from 2022.

SOUTHEASTERN

Another large franchise set to be replaced soon is Southeastern, which links Kent and south-east London with Victoria, London Bridge, Cannon Street and Charing Cross, and operates high-speed commuter services over High Speed 1 to London St Pancras.

To reduce overcrowding and cater for growing numbers of commuters from the region, the DfT has stipulated that the next franchise should add capacity for an extra 40,000 passengers per day by 2022. Although Southeastern operates a relatively modern fleet of EMUs, the oldest of which are the early-1990s vintage Class 465/466 'Networkers', it is widely expected that the next franchisee will place a large order for new commuter trains.

Interestingly, global transport giant Alstom announced in February that it had teamed up with Stagecoach Group to bid for Southeastern and would hold a 20% stake in the operation if the joint venture wins the competition.

"Our proposal aims to combine Alstom's knowledge of infrastructure and rolling

stock, with our operational expertise and customer service focus," said Stagecoach chief executive Martin Griffiths.

"The proposed arrangement supports our vision of delivering a more integrated and innovative rail service for the customers and local communities that depend on what is one of the busiest rail networks in the UK."

The other bidders, South Eastern Holdings, a joint venture of Abellio, East Japan Railway and Mitsui, and Govia – the current operator – in tandem with Keolis. The preferred bidder and its plans are currently expected to be revealed in November, with the new franchise due to start in April 2019.

NATIONWIDE NETWORK

Meanwhile, the race is also on to find the next holder of the CrossCountry (XC) network, which covers most of Britain, linking Cornwall with Aberdeen and Cardiff with Stansted Airport via a hub at Birmingham New Street and using parts of the West Coast, East Coast, Great Western

> Bi-mode trains could certainly prove their worth on the CrossCountry network, which is widely expected to see the unpopular 'Voyagers' replaced as part of the next franchise, due to be announced in August 2019.

and Midland main lines. Held by Arriva since 2007, the winner of the next franchise is due to be announced in August 2019 and the new arrangements will come into force next December.

Announcing the consultation on the future of the franchise, Secretary of State for Transport Chris Grayling stated that resolving overcrowding issues on the core sections of the XC network was the top priority for the next franchise. Various proposals are being put forward for this, but it is expected that new trains will play a part in expanding capacity.

Alstom is one of five companies shortlisted for the £2.75bn High Speed 2 train contract, which will be awarded in 2019. It is likely to offer a UK-compatible variant of its 'Avelia' family, developed from the hugely successful French TGV. ALSTOM

porterbrook

WEST COAST PARTNERSHIP

There is no clear view yet of what form this might take, but Bombardier's bi-mode inter-city 'Aventra' is one possible contender. Other sources suggest that locomotive-powered trains, such as the Stadler Class 68+Mk5a 'Nova 3' sets ordered by TransPennine Express could be in the running. True bi-mode trains could certainly prove their worth on this network, on which XC's Class 220/221 'Voyagers' and HSTs spend long periods running under the wires.

WEST COAST PARTNERSHIP

Preparations for the next West Coast Main Line franchise, which will include the design, development and introduction of the initial HS2 operation from 2026, are also well underway. Known as the West Coast Partnership (WCP), it will assume control of WCML services from April 2019. The bidders are all joint ventures, combining UK rail experience with international high-speed expertise. Shortlisted for the huge contract are First/Trenitalia, MTR of Hong Kong and China's Guangshen Railway Company (with Deloitte

trains capable of 225mph on the new line and working over the existing main line network north of Birmingham/Crewe.

Alstom, Bombardier, Hitachi Rail Europe, Siemens and Talgo were initially listed, although on July 4, 2018 Bombardier and Hitachi announced that they were joining forces and, if successful, would assemble the new 'British Bullet Train' fleet across its two UK factories. In response, the DfT added a second Spanish company, Construcciones y Auxiliar de Ferrocarriles (CAF) to the shortlist.

Alstom is expected to offer its 'Avelia' concept, derived from the hugely successful TGV family. Assembly would take place at Alstom's recently built facility near Widnes, Merseyside, which is currently refurbishing Virgin West Coast Class 390s.

Bombardier/Hitachi could offer a UK loading gauge version of their ETR 1000 'Frecciarossa' (Red Arrow), which is in service with Trenitalia and has been tested at up to 400kph in Italy.

A new entrant into the UK train market is Talgo, which is bidding for the HS2 contract with the innovative 'Avril UK', a development of its new Very High Speed Train for Spain. TALGO

> " The winner of the West Coast Partnership franchise will collaborate with HS2 Ltd to design, launch and operate the initial service and deliver a revised timetable on the West Coast Main Line to take advantage of the extra capacity provided by HS2. "

MCS, Panasonic Systems Europe, Snowfall AB, Trainline.com and WSP Parsons Brinkerhoff as sub-contractors) and a joint venture between Stagecoach, Virgin and French state operator SNCF.

The winning bidder will collaborate with HS2 Ltd to design, launch and operate the initial HS2 services and deliver the transition of the timetable on the West Coast Main Line as it is revised to take advantage of the extra capacity provided by HS2. As well as the £2.75 billion HS2 train contract (see below), this could also feature new inter-city trains for the classic WCML route. By the time Phase 1 of HS2 opens in 2026, the current Class 390 'Pendolino' fleet will be approaching 25 years old and could be a candidate for replacement.

However, the big train builders have their eyes firmly on the HS2 train contract and are already jostling for position.

In 2017, the DfT announced five companies had been shortlisted to build the fleet of at least 54

Karen Boswell, managing director of Hitachi Rail, said: "HS2 will form the backbone of Britain's future rail network and is a major investment in our future prosperity. Our partnership with Bombardier will draw on a huge wealth of UK experience and the best in modern technology – including our pioneering 'bullet train' experience. Our aim is to deliver a new British icon that will be recognised around the world – a Spitfire for the British railway."

Richard Hunter, managing director UK, Bombardier Transportation, added: "HS2 is a once-in-a-lifetime opportunity to transform the nation's transport network and we are very excited by the chance to play a key part in delivering it, and help generate skills and prosperity across a number of UK regions."

The two companies also worked together on a joint bid for the recent London Underground 'Deep Tube' contract won by Siemens.

The German giant is also keen to win the

The second Spanish train-builder vying for the HS2 contract is CAF, which was added to the shortlist in July 2018. It is offering its 'Oaris' concept, which has won orders from Spain and Norway so far. If CAF is successful, the trains will be built at its new factory in South Wales. CAF

porterbrook

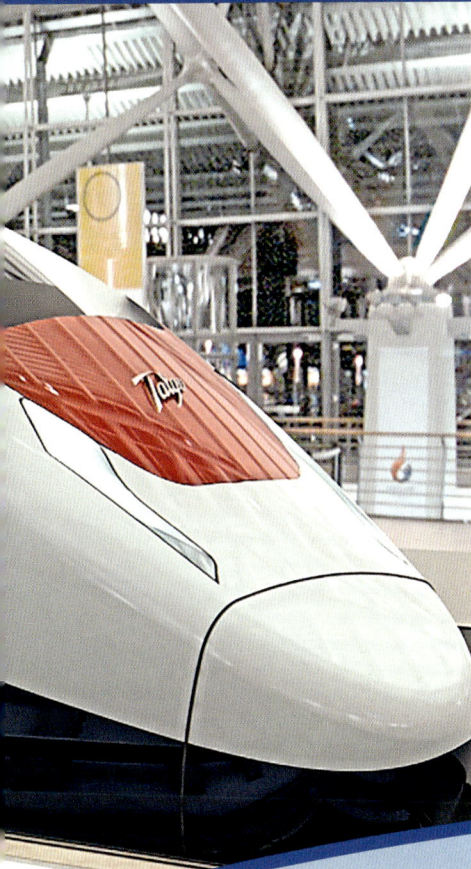

contract and is promising to build a UK train factory in Goole. Siemens, which announced its intention to merge its train-building business with Alstom in 2017, has signed a long-term agreement to lease a 67-acre site close to the M62 in Goole. It could invest up to £200 million in the factory, potentially creating up to 700 skilled engineering and manufacturing jobs, plus up to 250 construction jobs. Around 1700 indirect jobs could also be created throughout the UK supply chain.

The factory will build the new London Underground Piccadilly Line fleet, but could also assemble a British variant of the 'Velaro' very high-speed train (VHST) if Siemens is successful. 'Velaro' variants are currently in use in Germany, Spain, Turkey, Russia and with Eurostar on international routes from London. A new lightweight and cheaper version, the 'Velaro Novo' is also in development. Although it will be suitable for use on HS2, Siemens says it has no plans for a 'classic compatible' version for use off the dedicated high-speed route.

Also offering to build a UK factory to fulfil the HS2 order is Talgo of Spain, which has put forward a version of its new 'Avril' semi-articulated high-speed train. In true Talgo

tradition, the innovative design is quite unlike its more conventional rivals and promises to deliver greater capacity and lower operating costs – a claim that could prove irresistible to a DfT looking to maximise the number of seats per train.

Finally, the newest addition to the list, CAF, is also offering a version of a new design currently being built for Spanish high-speed lines. Welcoming their addition to the shortlist, Richard Garner, CAF UK director, said: "We are extremely pleased to be included in HS2's procurement programme. Our 'Oaris' high speed trains use the latest technology offering high speed travel that is comfortable, safe and provides digital connectivity to facilitate the busy world that we live in.

"The new high-speed trains will meet the highest international standards for passenger experience, noise reduction and environmental sustainability."

CAF plans to build the trains in its Newport manufacturing facility, which is expected to open in October.

The five bidders were invited to tender in summer 2018 and the DfT expects to award the lucrative, but challenging contract in 2019. The first pre-series trains will start to appear in the

early-2020s, allowing testing of the design and new high-speed infrastructure before the line opens in 2026. The successful bidder will also maintain the fleet from a dedicated rolling stock depot at Washwood Heath in Birmingham.

OTHER CONTRACTS

Looking further ahead, the sprawling and controversial Thameslink Southern Great Northern management contract currently held by Govia Thameslink Railway (GTR) is due to expire in 2021. Unless it is terminated early by the Government, the country's largest operator will continue to manage this enormous and complex network into the next decade.

Having endured years of disruption caused by the Thameslink Programme, industrial action, infrastructure failures and many other factors, TSGN is likely to be split back into its component parts. While Thameslink has a new fleet of Siemens Class 700s and Great Northern will have a mix of Class 365s, 387s and 717s, there will be some scope for new train orders for Southern when it is re-let. Although it operates a large and relatively uniform fleet of Class 377 'Electrostars' built between 2001 and 2014, it is also likely to be the last operator of 1970s-built 'PEP' family trains, retaining a fleet of 20 Class 313/2s (built 1976-77) at Brighton for the 'Coastway' route. These Beacon Rail-owned trains will be prime candidates for replacement under the next franchise. However, rather than new trains, Southern could be an ideal candidate to take on some of the relatively new EMUs being replaced on other parts of the network over the next few years.

Southern also leases a fleet of 20 Bombardier-built Class 171 'Turbostar' DMUs for the non-electrified London Bridge-Uckfield and Ashford-Hastings 'Marshlink' lines. Although pressure is growing to eliminate these diesel traction 'islands' from an otherwise all-electric railway, neither is likely to receive funding for electrification in the near future. Alternative options being considered are new bi-mode 750v DC third/diesel trains or the rebuilding of a small batch of

Porterbrook-owned Class 377s with an alternative power source – diesel engines or batteries – to allow them to work away from the third-rail and release the Class 171s (most of which are also owned by Porterbrook) to replace older DMUs elsewhere in the country.

MASS TRANSIT AND LIGHT RAIL

Away from the main line network, several systems are investing in replacement rail vehicles. The largest order of recent times was awarded to Siemens in June 2018. A total of 94 new 'Inspiro' trains will be built for London Underground's Piccadilly Line in a

> " Options being considered to eliminate Southern diesel operation include new bi-mode trains or the rebuilding of a small batch of Class 377s with an alternative power source - diesel engines or batteries. "

deal worth £1.5bn. The air-conditioned 'Deep Tube' trains will enter service between 2023 and 2026, replacing 86 trains dating from the mid-1970s. Up to 109 trains could eventually be built if options are taken up. Beyond that, Transport for London (TfL) is keen for all new 'Deep Tube' trains to come from a single supplier, so Siemens could eventually build up to 250 trains as part of the modernisation of the Piccadilly, Bakerloo, Central and Waterloo & City lines. All lines will use a combination of the new trains and modern automated signalling/control systems to increase capacity and frequency. Piccadilly Line frequencies are expected to rise from the

current 24 trains per hour (tph), to 27tph and, eventually, 33tph. Outside the capital, NEXUS, the public body that runs the Tyne & Wear Metro system, played host to a number of train manufacturers from around the world in June as it started the process to replace its Metrocar fleet.

A fleet of 84 new trains is being sought to replace the current fleet of 90, making use of increased reliability to maintain the present level of service. Nexus wants the new trains to improve passenger flow and reduce dwell times at stations, with features such as longitudinal seating, wider doors and standing areas, wider aisles and a layout to encourage passengers to move through the vehicle.

They should also be dual-voltage to operate on the Metro's 1.5kv DC electrification system and 25kv AC main line supply, which would allow an expansion of Metro services over under-utilised National Rail lines, such as the Blyth & Tyne freight line.

The successful bidder will be responsible for maintaining the current fleet of trains and to ensure there is a

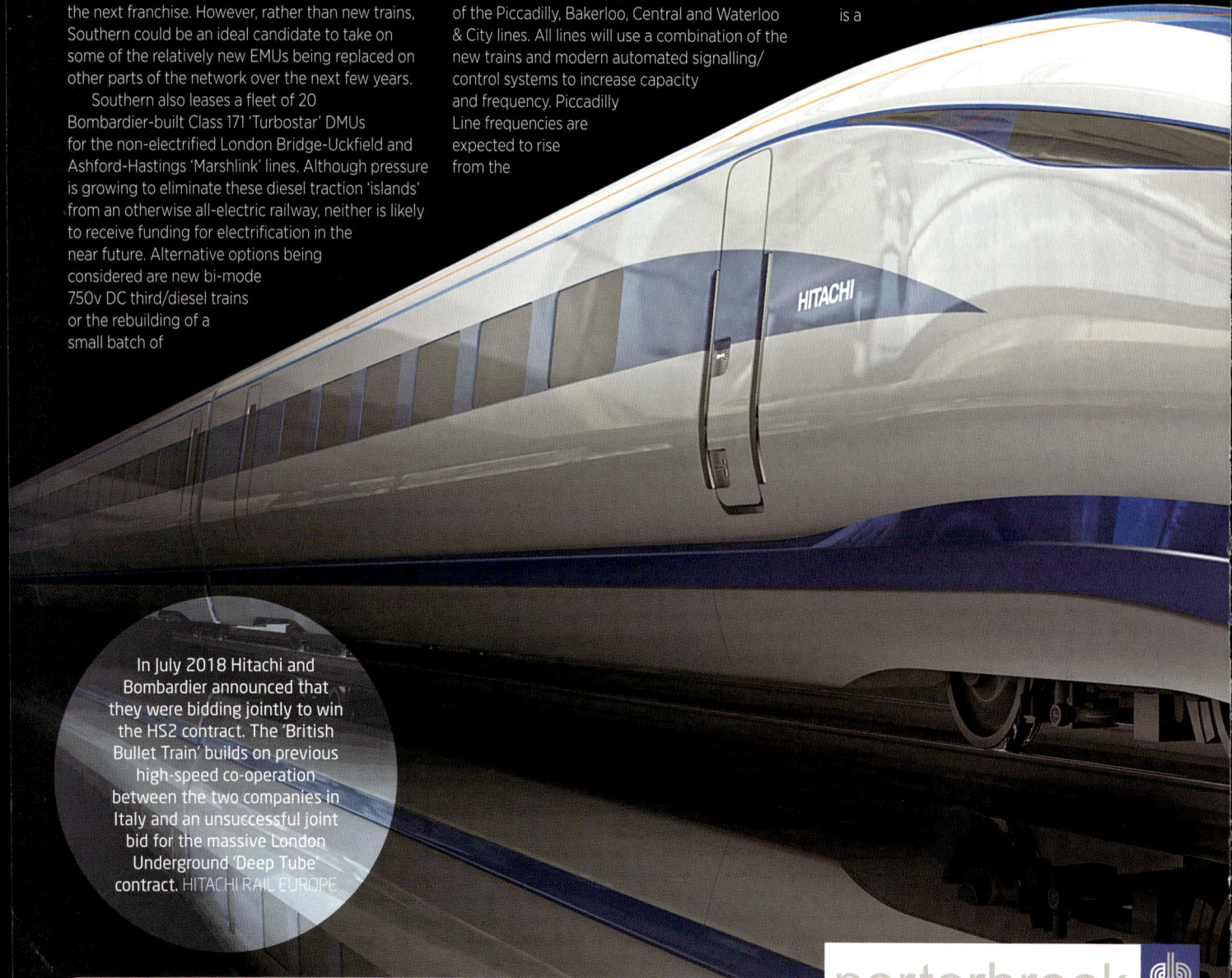

In July 2018 Hitachi and Bombardier announced that they were bidding jointly to win the HS2 contract. The 'British Bullet Train' builds on previous high-speed co-operation between the two companies in Italy and an unsuccessful joint bid for the massive London Underground 'Deep Tube' contract. HITACHI RAIL EUROPE

porterbrook

smooth transition between the old and new fleets.

Formal tender documents are due to be released at the end of the summer, with Nexus awarding the contract by the end of 2019 for entry into service in the early-2020s.

Stadler is in the process of building 17 new driverless trains for Glasgow's Subway. The £92m order was awarded by Strathclyde Passenger Transport in March 2016. Part of a £200m upgrade package won with Ansaldo STS, the trains will be Stadler's first for an automatic, driverless system and will be built at Altenrhein in Switzerland. The first trains should arrive in Scotland in 2019.

ALTERNATIVE FUELS

With public opinion increasingly turning against diesel, the Government has an ambition of banning diesel-powered road vehicles by 2040. This aspiration has been extended to rail vehicles and in early-2018 the DfT announced that diesel-only rail vehicles should be eliminated from the network by 2040. To many observers, that policy is at odds with the abandonment of the rolling electrification programme, but the Government is placing its faith in alternative 'clean' fuel sources – primarily batteries and hydrogen. Although these are yet to be tested in full passenger service, Alstom is investing heavily in the application of hydrogen technology to railway vehicles.

In Germany it has built two demonstration trains based on its 'LINT' diesel railcar product and has already secured

an order for 14 'Coradia iLINT' hydrogen-electric units from the Niedersachsen (Lower Saxony) regional government.

The UK is Europe's second-largest market for DMUs and with around 2400 trains set to become life-expired by the 2040 diesel deadline, Alstom sees great potential for its hydrogen trains in this country. In parallel with developments in Germany, the company is working with Eversholt Rail Leasing to convert a spare Class 321 EMU into a hydrogen-electric prototype. The four-car train will be fitted with storage tanks, batteries and fuel cells that convert hydrogen and oxygen into an electric current to power the traction motors.

Alstom and Eversholt aim to have the first modified trains in revenue earning service by 2021-22 and hope to secure contracts for a large fleet of hydrogen trains. Discussions are already underway with "a number of operators" according to Alstom. More than 100 Class 321/322 EMUs owned by Eversholt will be spare by the end of 2019, providing the potential for widespread deployment.

Other train builders and leasing companies, including Porterbrook, are also looking at hydrogen technology as an alternative fuel source.

However, one disadvantage of hydrogen is the significant investment required to build new infrastructure to support the fleet. While Germany still has substantial heavy industry producing hydrogen as a by-product, that is less common in the UK – although there are possible sources in the north-west and north-east of England. The gas can be produced by electrolysis using electricity from the National Grid, but that decreases efficiency levels and the 'clean' credentials of it as an energy source. Unlike diesel, it is not possible to deliver sufficient

quantities of hydrogen by road to depots, so trains will need to be based close to production facilities or pipelines constructed to deliver the gas. The German federal government is backing Alstom's 'iLINT' project with an £88m grant to cover the cost of building new facilities and supporters of hydrogen hope that similar support will be forthcoming in the UK.

Also attracting the interest of train builders is battery technology, which likewise has advantages and disadvantages over its rivals, although the cost, life and power potential of batteries is improving steadily. Vivarail is the first British train-builder to receive an order for hybrid diesel/battery trains, having sold five Class 230 trains to Transport for Wales in June 2018. It sees great potential for batteries, either as a standalone power source replenished by regenerative braking, charging points at strategic locations or in conjunction with diesel gensets or external electricity supplies. Battery-powered demonstration trains have been undertaking trials since 2017 and the first production battery set, No. 230002, is set for main line trials in late-2018.

Stadler is also offering battery technology on its 'FLIRT' multiple units and has secured orders from Transport for Wales for 24 tri-mode (diesel, 25kv AC and battery) sets for delivery in 2023. The trains will be able to operate in electric mode for up to 40 miles away from the wires, thanks to three large battery packs. The Swiss manufacturer will also install batteries on 36 'CityLink' hybrid train-trams for TfW (see page 82).

With air quality becoming an increasingly prominent issue for residents of urban centres and the politicians that represent them, it is clear that diesel's days are numbered and the development of new technologies will have to accelerate over the coming years to deliver trains that match the capability, range and operating convenience of diesel power. While the focus is currently on making passenger trains cleaner, the question remains of how hydrogen, batteries or other new power sources will be able to deliver the high power and long endurance required to replace diesel freight locomotives.

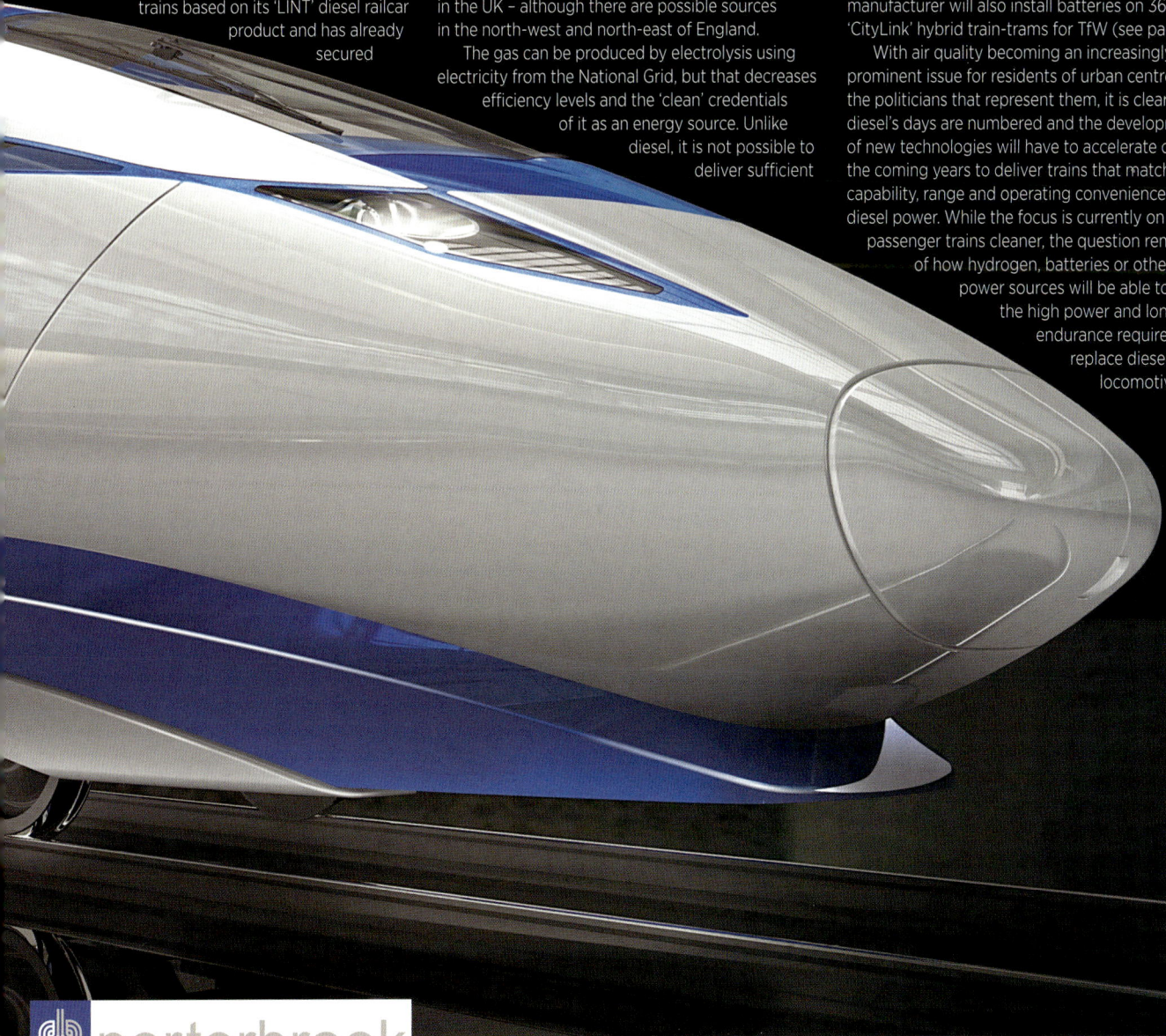

porterbrook

Since production of the EMD Class 66 ended in 2017, just two designs of new locomotives remain available to UK operators – both built by Stadler in Spain. Direct Rail Services (DRS) operates both types, the Class 68 diesel and Class 88 electro-diesel, leased from Beacon Rail Leasing.

DRS views the Class 88 as a true 'dual mode' locomotive, combining both 25kv AC electric and diesel-electric operating modes. It is a development of the Class 68 UKLight platform. Key features of Class 88 include 4MW AC traction equipment from ABB, a 700kW Caterpillar diesel engine for work away from overhead network, 317KN of tractive effort in both modes, nominal 100mph top speed, 500kW electric train supply rating and regenerative braking.

Class 88 shares many parts with the '68s', including bodyshell, cabs (the driver's environment has been developed together with union representatives), brake system, bogies, traction equipment and control software.

This new generation of dual-power locomotive is seen by DRS as highly flexible, with the ability to operate both heavy haul freight and high-speed passenger services, with self-rescue capability and flexibility to adapt to various passenger applications. The design also complies with the latest environmental targets (Euro IIIB on diesel mode).

porterbrook

Stadler Class 88

Operator:	Direct Rail Services
Built:	2016-17
Introduced:	July 2017
No. ordered:	10
Numbers:	88001-010
Order value:	Undisclosed
Routes:	Nationwide
Power supply:	25kv AC overhead/ Caterpillar C27 diesel engine
Max speed:	100mph
Power rating:	5360hp (electric), 950hp (diesel)
Features:	Last mile diesel capability, regenerative braking, electric train supply
Owner/finance:	Beacon Rail Leasing

One of 10 modern electro-diesel locomotives now in use with DRS, No. 88008 *Ariadne*, is off-loaded from the Eemslift Nelli at the Port of Workington on March 1, 2017. DAVE McALONE

porterbrook